Understanding the Internet

A Clear Guide to Internet Technologies

GW00566744

About the Author

The author is a Microsoft Certified Systems Engineer specialising in TCP/IP, IIS and SQL server. For the last 25 years he has been an independent consultant and lecturer working throughout the IT industry. As a result he has trained many thousands of industrial and commercial staff over that period. Currently, he divides his time between lecturing, consultancy and research work. He lives in the UK and travels worldwide for both business and pleasure. His client list includes many "blue-chip" companies together with government and international organisations.

Understanding the Internet

A Clear Guide to Internet Technologies

Keith Sutherland

OXFORD AUCKLAND BOSTON JOHANNESBURG MELBOURNE NEW DELHI

Butterworth-Heinemann
Linacre House, Jordan Hill, Oxford OX2 8DP
225 Wildwood Avenue, Woburn, MA 01801-2041
A division of Reed Educational and Professional Publishing Ltd

 A member of the Reed Elsevier plc group

First published 2000

© Keith Sutherland 2000

All rights reserved. No part of this publication may be reproduced in any material form (including photocopying or storing in any medium by electronic means and whether or not transiently or incidentally to some other use of this publication) without the written permission of the copyright holder except in accordance with the provisions of the Copyright, Designs and Patents Act 1988 or under the terms of a licence issued by the Copyright Licensing Agency Ltd, 90 Tottenham Court Road, London, England W1P 0LP. Applications for the copyright holder's written permission to reproduce any part of this publication should be addressed to the publishers

All trademarks referred to are acknowledged to be the property of their respective owners.

British Library Cataloguing in Publication Data
A catalogue record for this book is available from the British Library

ISBN 0 7506 4555 5

Produced by ReadyText, Bath, UK
Printed and bound in Great Britain by Biddles Ltd, *www.biddles.co.uk*

Contents

Butterworth-Heinemann/*Computer Weekly* Professional Series

Publisher

Mike Cash, Publisher, Butterworth-Heinemann

Series Editor

Dan Remenyi, Series Editor, MCIL (Management Centre International Limited)

Series Advisory Board

Frank Bannister, Trinity College Dublin
Diane Benjamin, National Health Service
Egon Berghout, Technical University of Delft
Ann Brown, City University Business School
Rodney Clark, Open University
Reet Cronk, University of Southern Queensland
Zahir Irani, Brunel University
Roger Lundegard, Applied Value Corporation
Arthur Money, Henley Management College
Chris Morse, FI Group
Tony Murphy, Gartner Group
Sue Nugus, MCIL
David Pennington, J Sainsbury plc
John Riley, Managing Editor, *Computer Weekly*
Mark Lewis, Management Editor, *Computer Weekly*
David Taylor, CERTUS
Terry White, AIS, Johannesburg

There are few professions which require as much continuous updating as that of the IT executive. Not only does the hardware and software scene change relentlessly, but also ideas about the actual management of the IT function are being continuously modified, updated and changed. Thus keeping abreast of what is going on is really a major task.

The Butterworth-Heinemann/*Computer Weekly* Professional Series has been created to assist IT executives keep up-to-date with the management ideas and issues of which they need to be aware.

Aims and objectives

One of the key objectives of the series is to reduce the time it takes for leading edge management ideas to move from the academic and consulting environments into the hands of the IT practitioner. Thus, this series employs appropriate technology to speed up the publishing process. Where appropriate some books are supported by CD-ROM or by additional information or templates located on the publisher's web site (http://www.bh.com).

This series provides IT professionals with an opportunity to build up a bookcase of easily accessible but detailed information on the important issues that they need to be aware of to successfully perform their jobs as they move into the new millenium.

Would you like to be part of this series?

Aspiring or already established authors are invited to get in touch with me if they would like to be published in this series:

Dr Dan Remenyi, Series Editor (Remenyi@compuserve.com)

Acknowledgements

My thanks to Mike Cash for his enthusiastic support of this book and all of the staff at Butterworth-Heinemann for their assistance. To my wife for her loyal, and often bemused encouragement over the "long nights" (When are we going to Oxford again?) and also to *Learning Tree International* (www.learningtree.com) for providing the best training courses on the planet. Once more I am indebted to Graham Douglas whose skill has turned my very rough diagrams and page layouts into something intelligible. Thanks to you all.

Why write this book?

The number of people and organisations connected to the Internet continues to grow at a phenomenal rate – partly fuelled by the availability of free Internet access. This explosive growth in usage is accompanied by a rapid expansion and evolution of the TCP/IP-based technologies on which the Internet is built.

This increasing complexity can make it difficult for the non-expert user to glean the basic principles on which the Internet operates. This book is my attempt to bridge that gap. It is aimed at the "typical" computer user wishing to make sense of the Internet – who wants to "peep behind the curtain" to get a feel for what's going on. I set out with the intention of providing an overview of "how it all works" and not to write a comprehensive reference for the IT professional. As such, some of the explanations will not satisfy the demands of the professional reader – who can find what they need in many of the excellent reference works available.

By keeping this book short and sacrificing some detail for the sake of clarity, I have tried to avoid deterring the casual reader from wanting to understand "the Internet revolution". Although the subject matter may change, the dilemma of just how much material an author should include is an ancient one, and a quote from 1000 years ago makes the point eloquently:

> *"We dare not lengthen this book much more, lest it be out of moderation and should stir up men's antipathy because of its size."*
>
> —Ælfric, schoolteacher of Cerne Abbas,
> then Abbot of Eynsham (c. 995–1020)

Chapter 1

TCP/IP, The Internet, Intranets and Extranets

A Short History of the Internet

Some parts of the following explanation have been simplified. As a result a few sections will not be as detailed as some readers would like. I make no apologies for this. There are many excellent textbooks that cover the fine detail. The purpose of this book is to provide a comprehensive "big picture" of the Internet and the technologies that underpin it.

What is all the noise about? Within the last few years everyone has been talking about the World Wide Web, and wide area networks. It seems that only a few months ago the information technology department was constantly pushing for local area networks and before that the mainframe always needed expanding. Why the sudden shift and is this simply a new fad?

The concept of the Internet started back in the late 1960s when part of the US Department of Defence was looking at ways of providing a "survivable" means of communication between different military bases. They wanted a relatively simple suite of programs that would enable communication to continue between different military sites in the event of a nuclear attack on the USA or any of its West European allies.

The concept was that there should be a variety of different lines of communication between different bases. If one base was destroyed then communication between the remaining bases would not be completely disrupted. This simple starting point rapidly developed from a fledgeling concept to, in the late 1970s, a relatively mature technology.

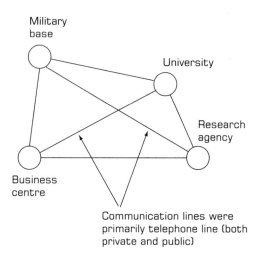

Figure 1.1
The fledgeling
Internet

The idea was simple but the software and technology, at the time, was considered leading-edge. Some of the universities were invited to join in the research and at the same time a new operating system started gaining acceptance amongst the university sites. This operating system was UNIX. Its major contribution to the early days of the Internet was that it came with a wide variety of communication programs built-in. As such it was a natural candidate for the communications-based fledgeling Internet.

So successful was UNIX at providing the bedrock computing for the early Internet that many of the supporting programs were written directly into the operating system and became an integral part of it. This position remained the case until quite recently.

There was only one problem with the assimilation of UNIX into the Internet. At the time (the mid-to-late 1970s) the UNIX world was largely populated by long-haired, sandal-wearing gurus and other enthusiasts. This was not quite the support population that the US military saw as the foundation for their communications project!

By the time UNIX was establishing itself, the principle of a flexible and survivable communication system had been proven. It was possible to provide a range of interconnecting computers and computer sites using standard telephone systems, microwaves, radio and so on and should one connection fail then communication could be relied on using one or more of the alternative paths.

The business community had started to see the possibilities for fast data transfer across multinational organisations and so a number of networks using similar principles and technologies were steadily developing. This network of networks formed the basis of what we now refer to as the Internet. Some of the networks are strictly military; some are for business; some for government use and some for private or local community use. All together they form what is now loosely called "The Internet". One of the main principles of this structure is the fact that communication between two computers can be achieved at the cost of a local call wherever those computers lie.

Does this mean we all get something for nothing? Well, yes and no. We all contribute to the infrastructure of the Internet through taxes (academic and military projects), through buying goods (business and research organisations) and through payments to our service providers – ISPs (Internet Service Providers). In all cases the actual charges are hidden or sufficiently small that on a session-by-session basis we do not notice.

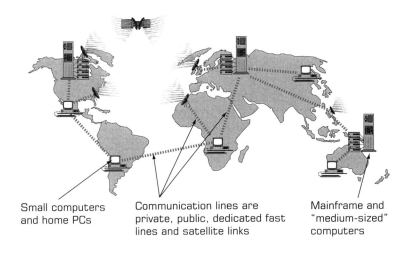

| Small computers and home PCs | Communication lines are private, public, dedicated fast lines and satellite links | Mainframe and "medium-sized" computers |

Figure 1.2   The modern Internet

TCP/IP

So successful was the early design for the suite of programs that formed the core components of the Internet that they have now become the most common method by which computers can communicate.

This suite of programs is collectively known as TCP/IP (Transmission

3

Control Protocol/Internet Protocol). Why the catchy name? Well the actual suite of programs is divided into four distinct groups of programs, each with a specific job to do. Prior to this design software tended to be developed as large "monolithic" programs. If one section had to be modified or changed it would be necessary to test and often rewrite the entire system. The Internet model provided a layered series of blocks of code. Each block would only communicate with the code immediately above or below itself. In this way the blocks of code were developed to be functionally separate from each other. One could be modified without those changes damaging the other blocks.

To see how this principle works imagine the way in which the MD of one corporation wishes to send some papers to his or her opposite number in another corporation (see Figure 1.3).

Figure 1.3
The layers

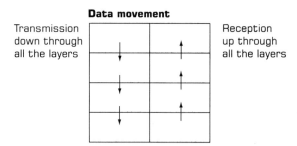

The computer model	The corporate model
Application layer (e-mail, FTP, the Web)	The Managing Director
Transport layer (TCP)	The Personal Assistant
Internet layer (IP)	The mail room
Network layer (Ethernet)	The courier

Data movement

Transmission down through all the layers

Reception up through all the layers

The first MD informs his or her PA that the papers are ready. The PA then contacts the internal mailroom staff who collect the papers internally and contact the courier service. The couriers come round to the building, collect the papers and take them to the receiving organisation. Here the same process is repeated but in the other direction.

If we think of TCP/IP as working in the same way, then we have a useful model to assist us. Starting at the top, with some e-mail, or a page from a browser, we have the MD. Next layer down we have the PA (TCP) and then the internal mail room (IP) and at the bottom is the courier (the wires, infrared, microwave and satellite transmission) which is the physical system that transfers the data. We see that components of the TCP/IP suite work in the same way as our simple organisation. Some of the programs provide an interface; some provide courier services; some provide checking facilities and some provide the general postal service. The important point is that one layer in the organisation only deals with the functional layers immediately above or below it. In this way the MDs of both companies are not concerned with which courier service is used only the fact that the packages are delivered on time.

There is no definitive set of TCP/IP programs. Different software manufacturers provide more or less of the entire available set of programs, depending on their perception of what is useful. There is a minimum set of programs which have to be provided before a company can state that it has a working TCP/IP system. This comprises a number of utilities and the essential components that allow the system to work.

Why all this talk about TCP/IP? Quite simply the evolution of the TCP/IP programs has meant that if a company wants to get two, or more, computers talking over just about any physical medium there is a version of TCP/IP that will let them do the job. Just like standard "house bricks", standard "screw threads" and standard "cassette tapes" TCP/IP provides a communication standard for computers. This standard applies whether those computers are based in the same room, the same building, the same state or county or the same planet. In all cases TCP/IP can be used to provide reliable, efficient and cost effective communication between computer systems.

Intranets

So, if TCP/IP provides the essential "building-blocks" of the Internet, what is an intranet? Quite simply an intranet is an internal network that uses the same software technology as the Internet – TCP/IP. In this way a small company-network gains all the benefits of the flexible, reliable, expandable network structure that is built into the Internet but for its own internal use. That company may, or may not, choose to connect their network to the Internet. In this way a company might decide to use TCP/IP for its own internal network as well as providing an in-house Web server (more on this term later) to make its product lists available to

5

prospective purchasers through the Internet. The company's Internet presence is very much like a shop window where a suitable range of goods is on display. There is nothing to stop the company providing a much more sophisticated Internet presence but for now we will stick to this simple example.

Extranets

An extranet is an intranet that is connected to the Internet but in such a way that some additional security has been built into the connections.

Figure 1.4
Intranets and
extranets

An intranet

All computers communicate using TCP/IP
but none have connections to the Internet

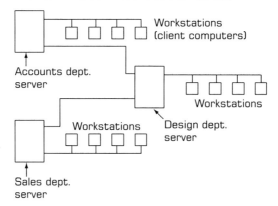

Workstations
(client computers)

Accounts dept.
server

Workstations

Workstations   Design dept.
server

Sales dept.
server

An extranet

Internal intranet technologies

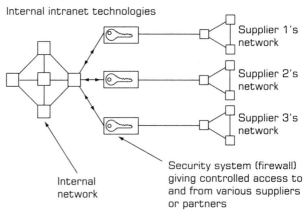

Supplier 1's
network

Supplier 2's
network

Supplier 3's
network

Security system (firewall)
giving controlled access to
and from various suppliers
or partners

Internal
network

In this design two regional offices of a company – say in New York and London – wish to be able to communicate with each other. They require more than standard e-mail systems and want the connections to be secure. They run TCP/IP over their internal networks and make their Web servers available over the Internet. For their own in-house purposes they provide a special secure connection between the two head offices. In-house staff can communicate with other staff over the more secure connection and also access the Internet. Outside users can contact the company's Web server but may not have access to any of the internal network. By using this method the company gains the use of the Internet and its associated cheaper long-distance connections without sacrificing the security requirements of the organisation. The alternative would often be the dedicated and much more expensive land line.

So that's all there is… we just use TCP/IP and off we go? In the same way that constructing a house requires more than ordering bricks and cement, preparing and planning for an intranet or extranet requires a little more thought.

Chapter 2

Names, Addresses and Name Resolution

Why do Computers Need Names?

Before computers on a network can communicate with each other they need to be able to *identify* and *recognise* other computers. This is achieved by giving each individual computer a *name*. In this context our definition of a network is two or more computers linked by a cable (or cables) which share data and communicate with each other.

The simple reason for the use of names is that at the lowest level the method by which computers communicate is pretty tedious for humans to remember. What is this method? On almost all networked computer systems the network card (the piece of equipment that prepares the data and messages for transmission across the cables) is identified by a unique number. This means that each and every card in the world has a distinct identification number. This number does not change and is assigned jointly by the card manufacturer and a centralised "steering" committee. (This is the theory, in practice some problems are caused by the fact that not all cards have *unique* addresses).

What does this unique number look like? Here are a few examples:

```
00 40 95 05 D3 8A
00 3C 00 03 A3 3D
00 10 4B 27 51 92
00 60 08 9A AD 05
```

These addresses are often referred to as hardware addresses or MAC (Media Access Control) addresses. This MAC address is used by computers to identify each other on a local network. By local network we mean all the computers on the same piece of cable or all computers in the same immediate locality. Normally this means a small number of computers in one room, floor or small building. (There are other considerations which we will discuss later).

MAC addresses are not the most memorable of number patterns to try to remember. If we were to use these numbers to communicate between computers the average user would get very confused and almost certainly give up. Unfortunately for us a number of computer manufacturers and computer-user organisations came up with a variety of solutions to these problems; two of the most common are outlined below.

Solution Number 1 – NetBIOS

Microsoft came up with a simplified method of identifying computers on a network. This method was called NetBIOS (Network Basic Input Output System). This method was simple, unsophisticated, relatively inefficient and quite noisy (more on this later). NetBIOS has recently come in for a considerable degree of criticism but when it was developed it represented an ideal solution to the problem of computers communicating on small networks. What do we mean by "small" networks? The original specification said that NetBIOS was suitable for computer systems linking between 2 and 20 computers.

The use of computers – even on small networks – has outgrown the modest plans of the developers of NetBIOS. Unfortunately, however relevant and well-planned the design may be, the ever-increasing demands of industry almost guarantee that shortcomings will be found at some point as the system goes through the expansion process and a much larger number of people use the system.

Even using the simplified NetBIOS naming system the underlying identification of computers is through their hardware or MAC address. The software that is used by a computer user hides this conversion process. In fact the name-to-MAC address conversion occurs quite often on a network and this allows the machines to communicate at the lower level. Normally all of this conversion process is hidden from the user.

What is a NetBIOS computer name? Quite simply it can be any "suitable" name up to 15 characters long. Some examples could be `mypc`, `workpc`, `gamews` or `finance1`.

In all cases the software will convert these machine names into the associated (unique) MAC address that is on the hardware card. As stated before this conversion is usually hidden from the user.

How does this work in practice? When you click on *Network Neighbourhood* or on any of the "network browsing systems" on a local network you almost certainly see a list of computers. These computers are identified by names. These names are the NetBIOS names and these have to be converted to the underlying MAC address before communication can take place. Please remember that here I am talking about browsing a *local* network. Browsing the Internet is a quite different process.

Figure 2.1
Computer name
to MAC address
translation

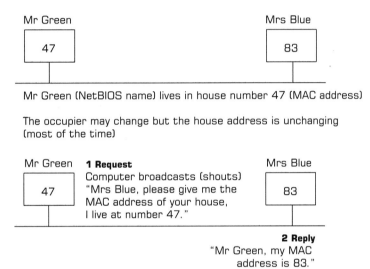

Mr Green (NetBIOS name) lives in house number 47 (MAC address)

The occupier may change but the house address is unchanging (most of the time)

Solution Number 2 – Domain Names

In the same way that NetBIOS names represent an improvement over MAC addresses, the designers of the Internet came up with both a numbering system and a naming convention which were intended to simplify the identification of computers on the Internet. The problems faced by the Internet's designers were considerably more complex than those faced by the designers of NetBIOS. The design complexities were primarily due to the size and structure of the Internet and the designers' wish to provide an expandable system.

The address of each computer on the Internet is unique. This address is also quite separate from the MAC address. Remember that MAC addresses are used to identify computers on a *local* network – i.e., all computers on the same network cable or in the same immediate loca-

11

tion. This is no good for the Internet which has computers spread over many hundreds (and thousands) of miles.

The Internet computer address is made up from four numbers arranged in what is referred to as "dotted decimal" notation. Here are some examples:

132.19.73.4
145.122.111.23
111.111.123.144

Again, each of these numbers identify a particular computer on the Internet but like the underlying MAC addresses they are not, for most people, very easy to remember. The Internet's designers came up with a naming convention that helps. This naming convention seems cumbersome at first but it has a structure that allows for expansion, flexibility and a reliable means of marrying-up the computer name with the underlying IP address.

Here is an example of a computer name from the Internet:

`mypc.xyzcompany.com`

This says that the computer `mypc` is in an organisation called `xyzcompany` and is part of a larger organisational structure called `com` (commercial). Here is another example:

`newpc.physics.londonuniversity.ac.uk`

This says that the computer `newpc` is part of the `physics` department in the London University (`londonuniversity`) organisation (or domain) which is in the academic centre (`ac`) of computer systems in the UK (`uk`).

The naming convention, as stated above, can be expanded and provides a reliable means of identifying computers on the Internet.

Summary

1. On a local network computers use a MAC address to identify each other and to transfer data between themselves.

2. MAC addresses are cumbersome. In one of the solutions to address this problem NetBIOS names are used to simplify (humanise) the process. Humans use the NetBIOS names and the computer software translates these into MAC addresses.

3. On a much larger network MAC addresses are inefficient and cannot be used. A more sophisticated address system has to be employed: this is the IP (Internet Protocol) address which is usually expressed in "dotted decimal" notation e.g., 144.19.72.4

4. The dotted decimal address format is confusing for humans so a structured naming convention is used for computers on the Internet. These names are called *domain names* and are of the form `mypc.finance.company.com`

5. Both NetBIOS names and IP (or domain) names, can co-exist and can often both be present on one computer.

Name Resolution

If we were to be content with quoting IP or MAC addresses at each other the system could have remained a lot simpler. Unfortunately, the introduction of the "humanised" names makes matters a lot more complex. With these "humanised" names we have to convert between them and their corresponding addresses. These conversion processes take up time, resources and introduce the potential for some serious problems. Why do we have to convert between the different types? Quite simply because at one level the computer uses the hardware address and at another level the user of the computer uses the more friendly name. The computer programs employed between these two extremes are busy converting from one form to another in order to maintain consistency and to give users the appearance of "seamless" connectivity.

The process of converting from a "humanised" name to a computer address is called *name resolution*.

From now on we will use the term "data delivery" or "delivers the data" to mean that one computer is communicating with another. This communication could mean sending some e-mail, moving some data from one machine to another or moving voice messages, pictures and so on between two computers.

Before we discuss the stages just remember:

*   All *local* delivery is via the MAC address (sometimes hidden by the NetBIOS name).
*   All *long-distance* delivery is via the IP address (and is eventually converted to the MAC address when the data reaches the target network).

- There is no simple relationship between the two addressing schemes *or* between the computer names and their corresponding addresses.

The stages in the process of name resolution are as follows:

- **For local delivery** The computer converts from the NetBIOS name or the IP address (they can both be present on a computer and used by different programs) to the MAC address and delivers the data locally.
- **For long-distance delivery** The computer converts from the domain name of mypc.work.com to IP address 111.123.121.11, delivers the data to the local network and then uses the MAC address for the final stage in the process. When delivering the data to the local network a number of stages might well be present. These stages, or "hops", are how the data can move round the world.

The more human analogy to this process would be that the domain name and IP address allow mail to move from sorting office to sorting office, or from railway station to railway station. MAC addresses function like the local postman – they get the data to the target address on the local system. The machines that act as these "sorting offices" are called *routers*. They route the data to the relevant network.

The system that computers use to identify domain names is called DNS (Domain Name System) from now on we will use the term "DNS name" and "domain name" interchangeably.

Some explanations of these addressing schemes have used the concept of a house number to represent the MAC address and the name of the family to represent the NetBIOS, or DNS, name. This suggests that the house number cannot change but the name of the family occupying the house may change over time. In the same way the MAC or hardware address rarely changes but the NetBIOS or DNS name might change over time. This may occur when a computer has new software installed or is moved from one company site to another.

Why is the system so complex and awkward? Quite simply we have three or four different technologies, developed at different times, to handle different tasks, and evolving at different rates that have now all been "made" to work together. The result is far from perfect. If we could stop the world and the development of electronics and computers for say, five years, then during that time it would be possible to put together a more comprehensive and cohesive system that is simpler and easier to use. Somehow I do not think that this will happen!

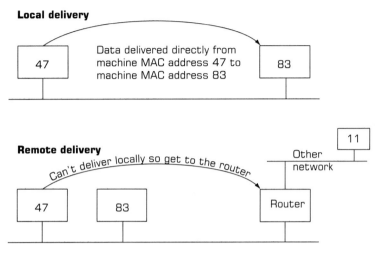

Machine (MAC address 47) tries to send data to machine
(MAC address 11) – which is not on the same network.
So the data is sent to the router which acts like the sorting
office and forwards the data to the relevant network.

Figure 2.2   Local and remote delivery

The situation that we now have is that there are two methods of naming computers and two different methods of identifying them by
address. MAC addresses are used for local delivery and IP (Internet Protocol) addresses are used for long-distance delivery. In almost all cases
the MAC address is hidden from users while they may be required to
enter the NetBIOS name or the full domain name as they copy data, use
printers or "surf" the Internet. The interaction between all of these systems cause many of the problems associated with the use of networks
and the use of some of the more general tools. We will discuss many of
these in the following chapters.

Chapter 3

DNS (Domain Name System)

Computer Names

We have seen that the confusing, numerical, addresses by which computers identify each other have be "humanised" is some way. The most straightforward way was to use a simple name for the computer. This is the method used by the NetBIOS system. This NetBIOS name, although simple, is based around an underlying process which is quite inefficient – especially for larger networks. We need to have another scheme that works better for these larger systems.

This naming system for larger networks was developed specifically for the Internet, which means it is efficient for large groups of computers and that it can be used as these networks grow even larger. Using this system a small company could implement the basic structure on its initial network and then grow this design as the company expands.

The Internet naming system is based on two principles:

1. Every machine on the Internet (or a corporate intranet) has a unique Internet Protocol (IP) address. (Remember this address is different to the hardware address used for local delivery of data). An IP address looks something like 123.19.74.13 or 167.133.16.121 and actually conveys two pieces of information: the network identification and the machine (computer) identification. These different components have the most general part on the left and the most specific part on the right. In the second example above, 121 could refer

to a particular computer on a network and 167.133.16 would refer to the network itself, whereas the address 146.133.121.177 could refer to network 146.133 and the computer on that network would be 121.177. The exact division of an IP address into the "network" component and the "computer" component is at the discretion of the network designer.

2. The IP address, although "friendlier" than the underlying MAC address, is still rather obscure and so we need to have a more "useable" naming system to identify the computer. The names that have evolved are usually something like this:

`mypc.mycompany.com` *or*
`thatpc.thatcompany.co.uk`

It is these rather daunting names that form the Web-page addresses that we type into our Web browsers. The general structure of these names is such that the more specific part of the name is on the left and the more general part of the name is on the right. This is the opposite of the IP address order and this difference will cause us a few problems later on. As an example, the name

`mypc.xyzcorp.com`

says `mypc` is a computer in a region (or domain) called `xyzcorp` and this is in the general region (or domain) called `com`; "com" is all of the commercial organisations in the Internet. The computer term used to represent all of the names in a particular system is the *Namespace*.

Imagine the overall structure, represented by the above name, as follows:

Figure 3.1
An Illustration of
the Namespace

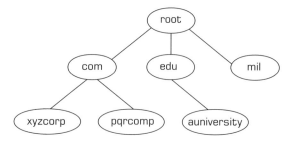

In Figure 3.1 both xyzcorp and pqrcomp are two organisations under the general control of the com domain. auniversity is one of the organisations which are part of the edu (educational) domain. The node called root is an administrative area that allows all the lower divisions to be organised in a unified way. In general, root is not used in day-to-day activities. In the real world there are many top-level domains and many thousands of companies under each of the first level groupings (com, edu, org).

To make things slightly more complicated the growth of the Internet has meant that the above structure is, in practice, no longer workable. The structure has become organised on a geographical basis along the following lines:

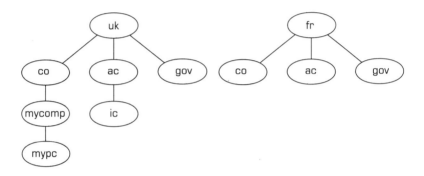

Figure 3.2   Recent changes in the Namespace

For example, ic.ac.uk is the Imperial College site (an academic centre (ac)) in the UK (uk) domain. mypc.mycomp.co.uk is the computer called mypc in the organisation mycomp in the co (commercial) domain in the UK.

This structure makes it easy to see the general type, complexity and simple structure of any organisation on the Internet, as long as the system designers have followed a logical and consistent naming convention. Unfortunately this is often not the case.

A major problem is that the IP address format 131.144.121.13 bears no natural relationship to this naming convention. This is just the way that the system has evolved. To convert from one to another we have to use a look-up table of one sort or another.

This table is similar in structure to a telephone directory with the name of the person we wish to contact on one side of the list and their telephone number on the other side of the list. In the early days of the Internet this was done by using a flat-file database system. A flat-file database is one whose data structure simply represents a list of information. Here is an example of the type of database that we are talking about:

Computer name	Computer IP address
mypc.mycompany.co.uk	101.12.132.144
fredspc.physics.ic.ac.uk	15.181.200.13
joespc.uscompany.com	115.12.111.146

And so on. Each row of this data table corresponds to the Internet computer name and its associated Internet protocol address (IP address).

In the early days of the Internet this list was quite short. With relatively few computers on the network the list did not need to be copied across to more than a few computers at any given time. As the number of computers grew and the rate at which new computers joined the system increased so the demands on this method of cross-referencing and looking-up computers became more and more unworkable. A new, more efficient, and more manageable means of controlling the list was needed.

To be able to provide a naming scheme that could cope with all the complexities of the growing Internet *and* provide some means of retaining a useable structure in the names posed a considerable challenge. The eventual solution to this was the *Domain Name System* or DNS

In DNS we have a naming system that is structured to mirror the physical layering of the computer systems on the Internet.

This is best illustrated by using a simple name and seeing how it fits in to the Internet model.

Structured Names

Let us imagine that we have formed a company called *Sportsco* which manufactures a range of sports equipment. It is early days and we have only just started but we have a unique product. This is a special type of training shoe that can be produced at a fraction of the cost of the competitor's shoes. We have decided that we want to market this primarily through the Internet and so one of our first requirements is that we establish a domain on the Internet (there are other ways of achieving the same end but our example will be used to illustrate the DNS concept).

We are going to locate ourselves in the USA and so our commercial company will come under the com domain. Our company's domain will reflect the name of the company and so part of our DNS name will be sportsco.com.

We only have three machines in our organisation (it is early days) and these are the finance computer, the general office computer and the sales computer. Using these functional titles – i.e. sales, finance and general – we have now got our three fully qualified domain names as follows:

```
sales.sportsco.com
finance.sportsco.com
office.sportsco.com
```

Each of these machines will need a valid IP address – which we will have to apply for (more details on this later). In addition, the machine that will act as our "bridge" to the Internet will also need a valid IP address. The structure of our organisation within the DNS hierarchy will look something like this:

Figure 3.3
Simple name
structure

Our `sportsco` computer will be directly connected to the Internet and will be a DNS server for our domain. Running a DNS server entails some administrative commitment. This commitment can be to the Internet (or an administrative body therein), or to our own organisation if we are running an intranet. So, what is the nature of this "administrative commitment"? Firstly, we will have to maintain a list of all machines in the next layer down in the domain that we are responsible for. In addition, we will have to inform other DNS servers about our own domain so that they know about us. Thirdly, we will have to know where to look if one of our computers needs to contact another computer outside our domain.

Let us take a simple example and suppose that we have been allocated the following IP addresses:

```
197.191.111.1
197.191.111.2
197.191.111.3
197.191.111.4
```

```
197.191.111.5
197.191.111.6
197.191.111.7
197.191.111.8
...
197.191.111.254
```

We have obtained these either from the central Internet administrative body or from our Internet Service Provider (ISP). We decide to allocate the numbers as follows

Computer name	IP address
sales.sportsco.com	197.191.111.2
finance.sportsco.com	197.191.111.3
office.sportsco.com	197.191.111.4

And our domain server (server.sportsco.com) is 197.191.111.1. On our server we will have to maintain a table of entries for our domain. This will look very like the simple list that we stated was too cumbersome for the entire Internet, but will work well for each of the smaller units which comprise the Internet. (There's only one way to eat an elephant... a piece at a time!)

Let us examine what happens when one of our machines needs to contact another. Suppose that sales.sportsco.com wants to contact finance.sportsco.com. The sales machine will look up the IP address from the server (server.sportsco.com) and this will return the correct IP address from its table. Once both machines have their valid IP addresses then they proceed to communicate with each other in the normal way (we will discuss this in detail a little later).

Let us expand our model a little more. Imagine that one of our suppliers has their own DNS domain. The diagram of the two companies looks like this:

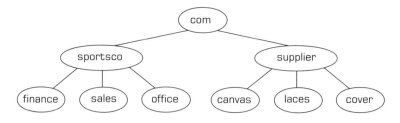

Figure 3.4   More complex name structure

Let us imagine that our machine `finance.sportsco.com` wants to connect with the machine `laces.supplier.com`. The general sequence of events would most probably follow those in Figure 3.5.

Returning to our Sportsco example; firstly, our machine `finance.sportsco.com` contacts its DNS server. This does not have the IP address of `canvas.supplier.com` and so it goes to the server at the top of the tree (`com`) and asks for the IP address of the `canvas.supplier.com` machine. The `com` server does not know this directly but directs the `sportsco` server to direct the request to the `supplier` server.

How does the `com` server know about the `supplier` server? Quite simply because as part of the DNS registration procedure the administrators of each level report their machine's name and IP address to the upper-level server. So the `com` server knows all about the servers "under" it. Since the individual computer names are relative to their position in the DNS "tree" the respective servers each step down through the name until they reach a server which has the required information.

Figure 3.5
How DNS
works

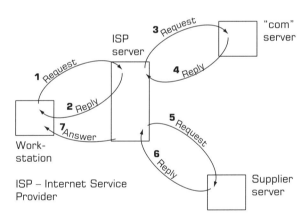

ISP – Internet Service
Provider

1 Give me the address of canvas.supplier.com
2 Please wait while I look it up. (The ISP server does not know the address but it knows the address of the ".com" server)
3 Give me the address of canvas.supplier.com
4 I don't know, but here is the address of supplier.com
5 Give me the address of canvas.supplier.com
6 Here it is 200.200.1.3
7 Here it is 200.200.1.3

The `supplier` server knows about all machines in its domain and so the address of the `canvas` machine is returned back along the request path.

In reality it is unlikely that all of the servers in a chain would be contacted. This is because DNS allows servers to cache (store) information that passes through them. In this way it is highly likely that one of the servers in a complex inquiry chain would know the target address and return this accordingly. A typical Internet Service Provider (ISP) will have a number of caching DNS servers at its site. The job of these servers will be to store (cache) IP addresses and their corresponding Fully Qualified Domain Names (FQDNs). This happens as the data passes back and forth when users make name requests of the different DNS servers.

Here we have used the term FQDN (Fully Qualified Domain Name). This is the correct technical term for a computer identified by its DNS name. We will continue to use the terms "domain name", "DNS name" and "FQDN" interchangeable since all are in common usage.

In the previous diagram we present the view from someone who is using their computer (possibly at home) and contacting, as their first contact with the Internet, the server of their Internet Service Provider (ISP). In the majority of cases this is the first point of contact with the Internet for most users. If we extend our Sportsco example a little more our client would be one of our staff who is trying to contact the Internet for some reason. The first server that they would contact would be the company server and this then assumes the same role as the ISP server in our example above.

Flexible Names

As our last scenario let us imagine that our Sportsco company has now grown and that we have three divisions, each with the department labels we previously used (see Figure 3.6).

Figure 3.6
The growing
company

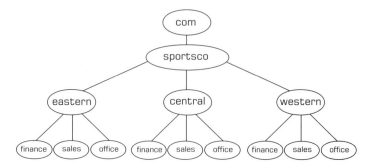

Now we have nine computers under three sub-domain servers all of which are under our main sportsco server. Each of the sub-domain servers knows all about the machines under them and our sportsco server knows about the sub-domain servers. It is now unnecessary for the sportsco server to know about all nine machines at the bottom of the tree. It has delegated some of its tasks to the sub-domain servers. We have the following machines all with their relevant IP addresses:

```
finance.eastern.sportsco.com    197.191.111.2
sales.eastern.sportsco.com      197.191.111.3
office.eastern.sportsco.com     197.191.111.4
...
sales.western.sportsco.com      197.191.111.8
office.western.sportsco.com     197.191.111.9
```

Clearly, we would need to have sufficient IP addresses to allocate to our rapidly-growing company. In actual fact the scheme outlined above would be flawed in practice. To understand this you would have to fully comprehend the subtleties of subnet addressing. This is outside the scope of this book and so the above example will suffice for the time being.

In this way we can have a combination of regional autonomy and centralised control.

It is unlikely that with only nine computers (workstations) in our company we would use the above structure but it illustrates the way in which DNS works. By scaling this up to the many thousands of servers in the Internet we can see the way in which the whole system works.

The major point to remember is that the data tables on each of the servers has to be entered manually. One of the main disadvantages of the DNS tables is that they are static. As the system changes then someone has to update the underlying data table. On a large, busy system this is no small feat.

If you have followed this discussion so far you may be thinking "What happens when systems change their addresses and other parts of their setup? Does the Internet contain vast tables of redundant data?" The answer to this is, generally, no it does not.

The various servers in the DNS scheme exchange data between themselves. Built into this data is a value called a *timeout*. This tells the receiving server to check the original server for updated information in a stated period of time. More simply it tells the receiving server to discard the data after a fixed period. The setting of these timeout values is carried out by the system administrators and is a balancing act between guaranteeing very accurate, or timely, data and the requirement of not saturating the Internet with vast amounts of data transfers. The result is, of course, a compromise. This is why occasionally when you try to contact a Web site you are informed "This Web site has moved" or "Web site cannot be found." This assumes that you have typed the name correctly!

Our previous explanation is a little simplified. In the actual DNS structure there is a "top level" of organisation called "root". The machines at the root level contain the names of all the DNS domains under them and these root servers act as the final arbiters in any name search requirement. In short, the root servers say "If you cannot sort out an address refer to me and I will direct you." At the time of writing there are 14 top-level (root) servers around the world. They are maintained by a mixture of governmental organisations, big business and academic centres. Figure 3.7 shows how they fit into our overall plan. Whenever you install a DNS server you will also install the IP addresses of these top-level DNS servers.

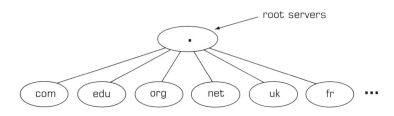

Figure 3.7   DNS root servers

The Lower-level Domains

A brief word about an older solution to the domain names problem. On some systems it is possible to enter a table of information containing a list of IP address and domain names directly into each individual machine. This table is a simple text-based file called "HOSTS". It was originally used on UNIX computers but can be found on almost any system that uses the TCP/IP protocols.

Although useful in some situations – and on smaller networks – it poses considerable administrative overhead when applied to larger networks. In general, it is better to use the centralised benefits of DNS rather than the distributed settings contained in the HOSTS file.

Chapter 4

WINS (Windows Internet Naming System)

More Computer Names

Throughout the earlier chapters we have stressed the fact that the two naming conventions (Fully Qualified Domain Names) and NetBIOS names have, eventually, to be converted to MAC addresses. Where FQDN names are concerned this is a two-stage process. Firstly, the FQDN is converted to the associated IP address by DNS (as we have seen earlier); this IP address is then converted to the MAC address using another program called ARP (Address Resolution Protocol). In the case of NetBIOS names the resolution is often done through a broadcast on the local network although other, more subtle, methods are available. To complete the jigsaw we may well want to convert our NetBIOS names into the associated IP addresses to allow us the simplicity of NetBIOS on a local network yet with all of the functionality of an IP based system for use on larger networks. By combining both name translation schemes together in all permutations we can have the best (and often the worst!) of all worlds.

We have seen that DNS replaced the need for the cumbersome flat-file database of all machine names to IP address mappings. With NetBIOS names providing the basis for almost all small computer networks, surely there must be some way of combining the two systems and thereby streamlining the NetBIOS name to IP resolution problem?

The answer to this is a definite Yes! The problem is that when we combine disparate technologies – which have evolved along separate paths –

we often pay a price in the complexity of the solution. So it is with the bringing together of NetBIOS and FQDN names and their associated IP addresses.

Just to recap. All computers use MAC (hardware) addresses to communicate locally. Most PCs use NetBIOS names as a way of identifying themselves in a more "human" way on a local network. We therefore need to be able to translate between the NetBIOS name and the MAC address. We also have the IP address to provide us with a means to transfer data over long distances and larger networks. In addition to the NetBIOS name we have a "larger model" name or Fully Qualified Domain Name (FQDN) that gives a more "human" means of identifying a computer than the underlying IP address. To "glue" this all together we need to translate between the FQDN and the IP address – performed by DNS – and also between the NetBIOS name and the IP address; the tool that does this is WINS. WINS (Windows Internet Naming System) was a development between Microsoft and the Internet Boards to solve the problem of NetBIOS name resolution on larger IP-address-based networks.

We have seen that DNS is based on a structured naming system and that its very organisation allows us to add sub-domains and additional computers quite easily. It has one major drawback – it uses *static* files. As such is can be a complex system to administer when one considers a network of the size of the Internet. Let us look at the problem.

Expanding the Business

Imagine we have started our small business and have decided to use Microsoft Windows as the main platform – for our current discussion it doesn't matter which version because they are all based on the same principles of name resolution. With our small network the concept of name resolution and all of the inherent strengths and weaknesses of each method of machine communication are hidden from us. It is only as the network grows that we start to have problems.

Imagine now that our business has grown and our network technicians are complaining that since we have divided our network into more manageable units (called subnets, more on this later) we have problems with some machines being invisible and other machines suffering from "broadcast storms". A broadcast storm is similar to being in a large room full of people where everyone tries to talk at once. As the noise level grows and they realise that they can't hear what the other person is saying they talk louder and more often until total chaos ensues. When the NetBIOS system was developed it was never intended for more than about 20 computers on simple network structures. So the principle of having the computers communicate by broadcasting (shouting to each other on the same subnet) was simple, effective and within the overall design (2 to 20 machines) easy to implement. This system breaks down on larger networks and networks connected to the Internet where many hundreds of thousands of computers (and often now millions) exist at any one time.

WINS provides a method whereby these problems can be overcome. There are other methods of solving the problem but in general these have been short-term solutions and all of them have a number of drawbacks.

WINS is quite simply a dynamic database that allows computers to register their NetBIOS names and their associated IP addresses. In addition it will answer requests from computers in its own – or another – subnet and is very successful at significantly reducing the amount of "noise" on a computer network.

Figure 4.1 shows the way in which computers communicate on a non-WINS network.

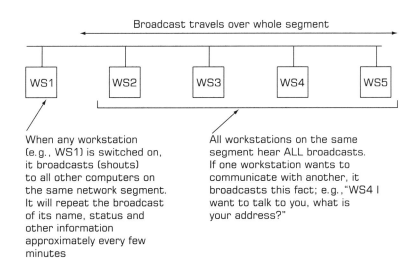

Figure 4.1 Diagram of machines broadcasting on a local network

And now for the WINS solution (see Figure 4.2). In Figure 4.2 Machine B is the WINS server. When switched on, Machine A (WS1) registers itself (NetBIOS name and IP address) with the WINS server. When Machine A wants to communicate with Machine C (WS4) instead of broadcasting it directs a specific request to Machine B which answers the request with the IP address of Machine C. Now that it has the IP address of Machine C, from this point on Machine A uses the normal methods (using IP) to communicate with Machine C.

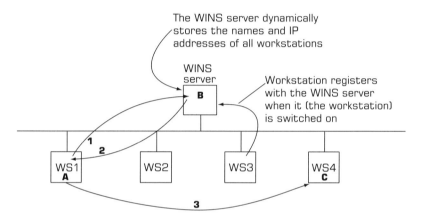

The WINS server dynamically stores the names and IP addresses of all workstations

WINS server

Workstation registers with the WINS server when it (the workstation) is switched on

If WS1 wants to communicate with WS4 it no longer needs to broadcast

1 It requests WS4's address from the WINS server
2 Assuming the server has this information, the details are returned to WS1
3 WS1 uses this information to communicate directly with WS4. No broadcasts are involved and much less network traffic is produced than with the original, broadcast, method

Figure 4.2   A WINS solution

With a more complex network structure we can use WINS to register computers and also to answer name requests.

One of WINS's great benefits is that it is a dynamic system. This means that when combined with DNS it can be used to provide dynamic registration of NetBIOS-based computers on a DNS-based network. All-in-all a much simpler and better way of working. Microsoft calls this system Dynamic DNS or DDNS.

With Windows 2000 Microsoft has implemented a newer version of Dynamic DNS. This uses the latest refinements to the DNS protocol and effectively has done away with WINS. It is still possible to implement an NT 2000 system in conjunction with the older NT 4.0 and WINS-based system but the amalgamation of the two does raise some design questions.

At the time of writing it is possible to do away with many of the problems of static name registration by using a WINS-based system or in the future by implementing an Windows 2000-based network. This reduces the administrative overhead required and also removes some of the scope for errors to be introduced into the system by incorrect entries being entered into the DNS tables.

Chapter 5

FTP (File Transfer Protocol)

Moving Data Around the World

In the early days of the Internet users had two main requirements: electronic mail and file transfer. Today, these two activities still account for a major proportion of Internet use.

FTP (File Transfer Protocol) was the original method by which files could be transferred from one computer to the other. Traditionally, FTP used a command line interface. This type of interface is familiar to DOS or UNIX users.[1] Now most FTP systems hide the command line interface behind some sort of "easy-to-use" graphical interface. Whichever method your system uses, the principles are the same.

If your company wants to transfer large programs or data files from one site to another it will be necessary to use either FTP by itself or to use some extensions to the e-mail (electronic mail) facility. We will be looking at e-mail and the associated programs in a later chapter.

Let us go back to our sample fledgling company Sportsco. We are designing our Internet connection. What do we need to do to use FTP on our site? And, more importantly, do we need to consider using FTP. If we want to make files, data or programs available to outside users we will need to have use of an FTP server. Typically this is a computer designated to providing access to part of its file structure (often called the file system) to remote users. There are three main ways to provide FTP serv-

---

1. DOS and UNIX are two popular operating systems that predate Windows; they are notorious for being user "hostile" but, in the case of UNIX, the gurus love them.

ers. These are UNIX-based systems; Novell-based systems and systems using Microsoft IIS (Internet Information Server). There are many smaller (and often excellent) solutions available but these three form the main group of products. In most of the following discussions and examples we will be using the Microsoft product as an illustration.

The latest version of IIS provides both Web server capabilities (more on this later) and FTP server capabilities.

We could integrate our FTP server into our corporate network and use this to allow users to connect to us. A typical way in which this might be done is shown in Figure 5.1.

Figure 5.1
The layout of the new Sportsco domain including the FTP server at 197.191.111.200

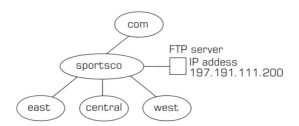

Users could now connect to our server by accessing the machine ftp.sportsco.com. This would connect them to our server. In this book when we talk about a "server" we simply mean a computer that offers part of its resources to other computers on the network. These resources can be files, folders (or directories), printers or other parts of the computer system. The network can be a small local one or a larger network such as the Internet. In the above example this connection could be made by using the Web browser or by a command-line interface. This latter option is becoming increasingly rare as more and more users utilize the flexibility and ease of use of the Web browser.

> **Warning**
> It is vital that when setting up the FTP server that due attention is given to security. It is possible for knowledgeable users to "hack" through the default security on many systems. In general, the setting up of Internet-connected networks is best left to trained professionals rather than a "try it and see" approach. An incorrectly secured network or incorrectly secured FTP server can give total access to a company's data and computer resources. If you are not absolutely sure about your site's security assume that the data is visible to the outside world. A suitable discussion of this topic is outside the scope of this book.

Modern Implementations

As stated above, most modern Web browsers (Internet Explorer or Netscape Navigator) can give access to FTP sites. Old hands may still prefer the command-line interface to access the FTP server. Most systems now provide a suitable GUI (Graphical User Interface) based FTP tool to allow the user to either upload files (copy them to the server from the user's computer) or download files (copy them from the FTP server to the user's computer).

If we were to look at the way in which a user would interact with an FTP site we would see a series of commands like GET and PUT together with the usual "command line" instructions that we associate with the DOS or UNIX operating systems. Many software vendors have added a more "friendly" user interface to their FTP programs but essentially the system remains the same: you upload or download files to and from a server either by using the command line or by using the graphical equivalent. In spite of the success of the Web, FTP still remains a very efficient method of moving large files around the Internet and FTP servers look like being with us for some time. The following screenshots show a typical command line FTP session (Figures 5.2 to 5.4) and a sample Web-browser-based FTP session (Figure 5.5).

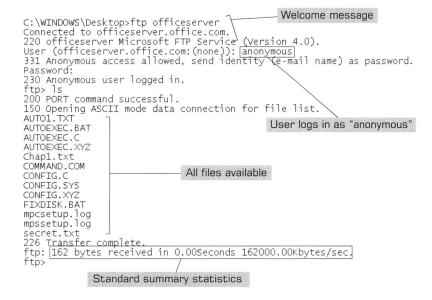

Figure 5.2   Text-based FTP (1)

When looking at Figures 5.2 to 5.4, see how cluttered and "busy" the screens are – and this is a simple example! This is one of the reasons why the early Internet had such a daunting reputation – particularly for novice users.

```
C:\WINDOWS\Desktop>ftp officeserver
Connected to officeserver.office.com.
220 officeserver Microsoft FTP Service (Version 4.0).
User (officeserver.office.com:(none)): anonymous
331 Anonymous access allowed, send identity (e-mail name) as password.
Password:
230 Anonymous user logged in.
ftp> ls
200 PORT command successful.
150 Opening ASCII mode data connection for file list.
AUTO1.TXT
AUTOEXEC.BAT
AUTOEXEC.C
AUTOEXEC.XYZ
Chap1.txt
COMMAND.COM
CONFIG.C
CONFIG.SYS
CONFIG.XYZ
FIXDISK.BAT
mpcsetup.log
mpssetup.log
secret.txt
226 Transfer complete.
ftp: 162 bytes received in 0.00Seconds 162000.00Kbytes/sec.
ftp> ls -l
200 PORT command successful.
150 Opening ASCII mode data connection for /bin/ls.
-r-xr-xr-x   1 owner    group           2006 Sep 28  1996 AUTO1.TXT
-r-xr-xr-x   1 owner    group            144 May 10 10:09 AUTOEXEC.BAT
-r-xr-xr-x   1 owner    group            140 Dec 18  1995 AUTOEXEC.C
-r-xr-xr-x   1 owner    group           2006 Sep 28  1996 AUTOEXEC.XYZ
-r-xr-xr-x   1 owner    group          10247 Sep  1 16:53 Chap1.txt
-r-xr-xr-x   1 owner    group          54645 May 31  1994 COMMAND.COM
-r-xr-xr-x   1 owner    group            360 Sep 28  1996 CONFIG.C
-r-xr-xr-x   1 owner    group             71 Feb  9 21:42 CONFIG.SYS
-r-xr-xr-x   1 owner    group            311 Sep 27  1996 CONFIG.XYZ
-r-xr-xr-x   1 owner    group            109 Dec 18  1995 FIXDISK.BAT
-r-xr-xr-x   1 owner    group           1835 Feb 10 13:08 mpcsetup.log
-r-xr-xr-x   1 owner    group          16541 Feb 10 13:01 mpssetup.log
-r-xr-xr-x   1 owner    group             39 Apr 26 12:14 secret.txt
226 Transfer complete.
ftp: 929 bytes received in 0.06Seconds 15.48Kbytes/sec.
ftp> get secret.txt
200 PORT command successful.
150 Opening ASCII mode data connection for secret.txt(39 bytes).
226 Transfer complete.
ftp: 39 bytes received in 0.11Seconds 0.35Kbytes/sec.
ftp>
```

Command to copy the document

More detailed listings use UNIX-like commands

Figure 5.3 Text-based FTP (2)

```
220 officeserver Microsoft FTP Service (Version 4.0).
User (officeserver.office.com:(none)): anonymous
331 Anonymous access allowed, send identity (e-mail name) as password.
Password:
230 Anonymous user logged in.
ftp> ls
200 PORT command successful.
150 Opening ASCII mode data connection for file list.
AUTO1.TXT
AUTOEXEC.BAT
AUTOEXEC.C
AUTOEXEC.XYZ
Chap1.txt
COMMAND.COM
CONFIG.C
CONFIG.SYS
CONFIG.XYZ
FIXDISK.BAT
mpcsetup.log
mpssetup.log
secret.txt
226 Transfer complete.
ftp: 162 bytes received in 0.00Seconds 162000.00Kbytes/sec.
ftp> ls -l
200 PORT command successful.
150 Opening ASCII mode data connection for /bin/ls.
-r-xr-xr-x   1 owner    group              2006 Sep 28  1996 AUTO1.TXT
-r-xr-xr-x   1 owner    group               144 May 10 10:09 AUTOEXEC.BAT
-r-xr-xr-x   1 owner    group               140 Dec 18  1995 AUTOEXEC.C
-r-xr-xr-x   1 owner    group              2006 Sep 28  1996 AUTOEXEC.XYZ
-r-xr-xr-x   1 owner    group             10247 Sep  1 16:53 Chap1.txt
-r-xr-xr-x   1 owner    group             54645 May 31  1994 COMMAND.COM
-r-xr-xr-x   1 owner    group               360 Sep 28  1996 CONFIG.C
-r-xr-xr-x   1 owner    group                71 Feb  9 21:42 CONFIG.SYS
-r-xr-xr-x   1 owner    group               311 Sep 27  1996 CONFIG.XYZ
-r-xr-xr-x   1 owner    group               109 Dec 18  1995 FIXDISK.BAT
-r-xr-xr-x   1 owner    group              1835 Feb 10 13:08 mpcsetup.log
-r-xr-xr-x   1 owner    group             16541 Feb 10 13:01 mpssetup.log
-r-xr-xr-x   1 owner    group                39 Apr 26 12:14 secret.txt
226 Transfer complete.
ftp: 929 bytes received in 0.06Seconds 15.48Kbytes/sec.
ftp> get secret.txt
200 PORT command successful.
150 Opening ASCII mode data connection for secret.txt(39 bytes).
226 Transfer complete.
ftp: 39 bytes received in 0.11Seconds 0.35Kbytes/sec.
ftp> bye
221

C:\WINDOWS\Desktop>
```

Command to
close the session

Figure 5.4   Closing the connection

37

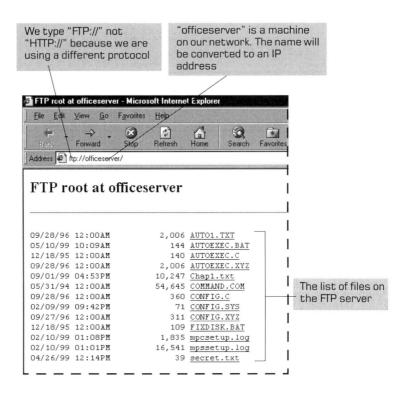

Figure 5.5 Graphical-based FTP

Chapter 6

The World Wide Web

Flexible Documents

The World Wide Web (or WWW) is what most people think of as "The Internet". In fact, the Web is one of the most recent additions to the Internet. Why, then, has it become synonymous with the Internet? The answer is quite simple. The interface (the method of access) that the Web uses is sufficiently "user friendly" to make even the most delicate computer novice feel that they are using something like an intuitive "question and answer" document. Although this is true for the interface the same cannot be said of the technology on which the Web is based. Due to demand this technology is frequently perceived to be "creaking at the seams" and often this is not far from the truth.

The protocol on which the Web is based was initially devised by a British scientist, Tim Berners-Lee, working at the nuclear research centre at CERN[1] in Switzerland. His requirement was for something that would allow the transport of documents and graphics in an easy to use format rather than the slightly cumbersome methods employed by the various FTP systems. While FTP was good enough for large files and programs it provided too much "overkill" for the transmission of documents and their associated graphics files.

The basis of the Web is that documents are created using a special markup language. With this certain standard commands are embedded

---

1. Conseil Européen pour la Recherche Nucléaire.

in documents to enable them to represent their contents in a particular way. For example the command <title1> could refer to a line of text which was to be printed in a large typeface in bold and centered in the middle of a page. This type of document and the particular markup language is now referred to as HTML (HyperText Markup Language).

A sample HTML page is shown in Figure 6.1.

```
<html>

<HEAD>
    <TITLE>Fantastic Demonstration</TITLE>
</HEAD>

<BODY>

<H1>Hello Readers</H1>
    This is a short demonstration of HTML commands.
    It is meant to demonstrate how a WEB page is constructed.

<P>
    This is another paragraph.
    For more information you can contact the following site
    (This is not a real location!!!!)
    <A Href="http://www.sportsco.co.uk/html/">
    www.sportsco.co.uk/html</A>

<P>
    <ADDRESS>
    <A HREF="http://www.sportsco.co.uk/fred/">Fred Grummitt</A>
    (Fred@sportsco.co.uk) /10 May 1999-09-02
    </ADDRESS>

</BODY>

</HTML>
```

Commands to begin and end the title for the page

The begin and end heading command

The textual prompt that will refer to (**A**)

A reference to another Web site (**A**)

Figure 6.1   Simple HTML. Note: "◄┘" indicates text which had to wrap onto the next line because it was too long to display here. In an actual HTML file it would appear as a single line.

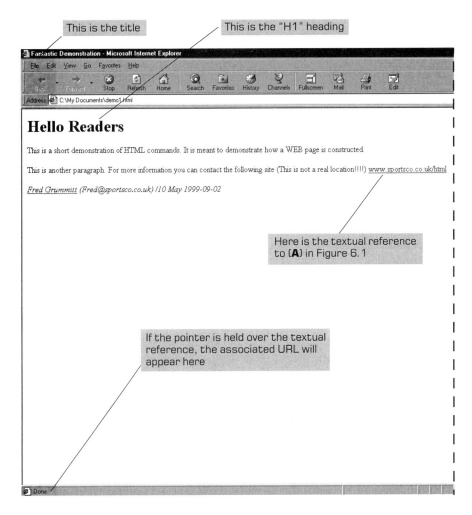

Figure 6.2 How Figure 6.1 looks when viewed through a browser

The most common way in which this is used is for one computer user (the client) to access data on another computer (the server). These two computers can be in the same location, in the same area or in different parts of the world. All that is required is that the computers use TCP/IP to communicate and that they have access to the Internet. For a specific company these machines could all be "in-house" and be used to produce an internal "bulletin board". If the Web server is not required to be accessed from outside the company all that is needed is that the internal network uses the TCP/IP protocol and that the users know the FQDN of the associated Web server.

Other markup commands, similar to those used in our simple example, arrange lists, produce boxes and other enhancements on the page. One of the most important concepts introduced by HTML was that of the *hyperlink*. In this an explicit reference could be made to another document stored on the same computer or on another computer on the other side of the world.

Joining Documents

How is this done? Quite simply by the fact that the hyperlink uses either the FQDN (Fully Qualified Domain Name) or the IP (Internet Protocol) address of the target computer and then refers to the desired document on the target computer inside this reference.

In this way, a reference to the Web server (a computer dedicated to making Web pages available to Internet users) for Sportsco's eastern site would be something like this:

```
http://www.sportsco.eastern.com
```

This direction command would be embedded into a document using the correct HTML tags – by the designer of the Web page. Then when the user clicked on this reference using the mouse, the client computer would look up the IP address of sportsco.eastern.com and having found the correct IP address would contact the associated Web server and try to load the default page on that server.

Let us imagine that the server held a price list for our target company and that we wanted to get the latest prices from that server. It could be that the person(s) building the eastern Web server had decided to place all price information in a directory called prices. Inside this directory would be a number of documents linked by hyperlinks. One of them could contain the most up-to-date price information. This document will be called latest. The command to access this from our Web document would be something like this:

```
http://www.sportsco.eastern.com/prices/latest.htm
```

Having got the latest prices off of the server the client adds a bookmark or a favourite site into the Web browser. Whenever they want the latest prices, clients (users) just click on this reference; the target computer is contacted and the new price list is displayed.

The beauty of this arrangement is that on the bookmark, or Web page, stored on the client computer the above reference to the target computer stays the same. From one week to the next when our user wants to contact the eastern Web server all they have to do is to click on the relevant part of the page and the system looks up the eastern server as before.

When the staff at the eastern server have a new price list, they simply copy the new HTML document onto the relevant directory on the server and the file is then available to anyone who is allowed to access it. In many situations this copy arrangement could be automated from the database or whatever software produces the price list. The following two diagrams illustrate this.

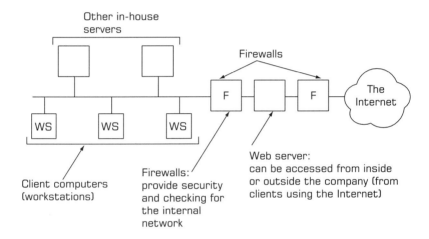

Figure 6.3   The Internet/extranet setup

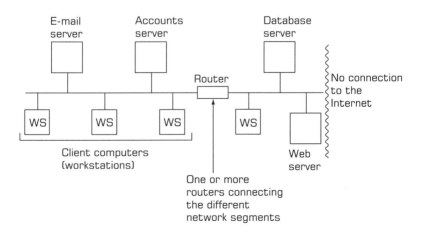

Figure 6.4   The intranet setup

Clearly, the programs that are used to access the Web server need to be able to interpret the HTML commands and also to lookup the relevant IP addresses from whichever DNS servers are being used. The requirements made by these demands led to the development of specialist software called *Web browsers*. Originally there were a number of different versions of general browser software, including some proprietary ones. Nowadays these have almost all been superseded by two browsers: Netscape's Navigator (now usually called Netscape Communicator) and Microsoft's Internet Explorer.

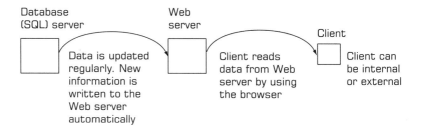

Figure 6.5   Automatic site update

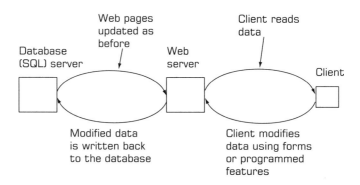

Figure 6.6   Automatic updates with client modifications

Each of these two tools has its advocates and the argument rages back and forth as to which is the best/fastest/easiest to use and so on. In fact they are very similar in overall performance and general use. Navigator is the most common throughout most of North America and Explorer predominates in Europe.

The range of browsers historically in use can affect the design considerations of a company planning to implement their own Web site. In this case the only real consideration for a company planning to develop its own Web site, either for internal or external use, is that the Web pages being developed on the server need to be able to be read by as many of the standard browsers as possible. This normally means both Navigator and Explorer. The specialist features found in each should be used sparingly and an alternative method of displaying information should be provided so that users of the other browser will not just get a blank document presented in front of them. Most of the Web-site development software can automatically adjust the content to fit in with either of the browsers. This can mean that a site has to maintain two sets of HTML documents.

The browsers have a range of standard features. They all let you select an HTML page, search the Internet for text, subjects, diagrams and so on and also save information to disk. In addition, they will allow you to store a list of commonly accessed Web servers (or sites) and may allow customisation of things like security, colours and other "environmental" variables.

Figure 6.7 shows a sample session from Microsoft's Internet Explorer. The Web site that has been accessed here is one of the BBC's excellent examples of good Web design.

Figure 6.8 is a sample page from a Netscape Navigator session (now Netscape Communicator). This is again the BBC site and it shows the overall similarities between the two browser systems.

Increasingly, Web sites are becoming the preferred format used by organisations to provide details of their company's products or range of services. A well-designed Web site can attract and assist customers to locate products or information and to make purchasing decisions that can directly affect profitability. By contrast, a poorly-designed site can turn potential customers away and have a strongly negative effect on "corporate image".

Many organisations are now choosing to publish their support material in HTML format. The advantage, to the organisation, of this approach is that once the source material has been produced it can be made available electronically either locally on the company's Web server, on a CD for distribution to clients, or across the Internet. The same source materials can be used to produce the "traditional" hard copy books should this be required. This electronic publishing can be very cost-effective as a way of making a company's published products available to the public. In a recent announcement the publishers of The

Figure 6.7   The BBC's Web site displayed with Internet Explorer

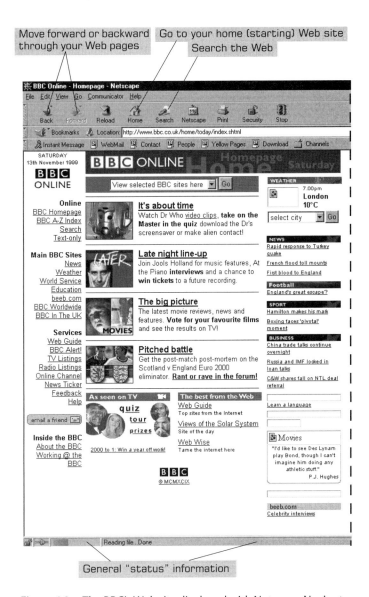

Figure 6.8   The BBC's Web site displayed with Netscape Navigator

Encyclopaedia Britannica stated that they are no longer going to be producing the encyclopaedia in "hard copy" (on paper) but that it will only be available on CD. They quote cost of printing and ease of updates as the two major reasons for this decision.

Over the next few years we can expect many more organisations producing such "traditional" products to come to the same conclusion. This will reduce publication, distribution and update costs but will mean that access to such sources of reference will only be possible for people with the necessary technical skills and computer hardware.

As you can see from the above two examples the browsers are very similar. The functions to which they are put are identical and either serves as a valid method for accessing Web-based data from either an intranet-, Internet- or extranet-based system.

How do browsers get information from the underlying servers? This is the topic that we will look at now.

One of the important things to bear in mind when discussing how Web browsers and Web servers interoperate is that the initial designs (on which most of the current systems are based) were intended to provide access to far less complex documents and far smaller amounts of data than is now the case. As ever, modern demands have greatly exceeded the original specification; as a result of this, overall system performance has been adversely affected.

URLs

When discussing the way in which a browser contacts a server and gets data from it, we will use the simple illustration of someone trying to contact a remote Web server to download (access) some data.

The steps in the process are as follows. On the client machine (the one where the user is sitting) the user types in a URL (Uniform Resource Locator) name. This is of the form:

```
http://www.microsoft.com
```

What does this tell us? The http component says that we are going to use the HyperText Transfer Protocol to communicate. This allows the two computers at either end of the connection to ascertain which language they are going to use to communicate with each other. (Although most systems will use HTTP there are some other options and in the future more will be added.) One of the newer ones is HTTPS which is a secure HTTP system. This will be used for any data transfer where some degree of security and/or control is required.

Following on from the http part of our URL are the:// characters. This is simply some syntax to allow the computers to separate the language specification part of the URL from the FQDN (Fully Qualified Domain Name) component.

After the:// comes the FQDN (www.microsoft.com) which says that we want to contact the Web server of Microsoft and that this server is in the com (commercial organisation) domain. This server is physically located in America.

How does our machine contact the Web server? First it needs to know the IP (Internet Protocol) address of the Web server; but where does it get this?

In the initial connection process our machine will most likely contact the server of our Internet Service Provider (ISP). This will be someone like America OnLine (AOL), CompuServe, BT, AT&T or any of the many other providers. These companies have their servers scattered around the world and in most cases our user will contact them using only a local telephone call.

Our user's machine knows how to contact the ISP because the software that will have been installed onto the user's computer by the ISP will have set this up (usually automatically).

Once contacted, the ISP server may well know the IP address of the Microsoft server – but how does this happen? Most servers around the world provide the ability to cache (store) IP addresses that have been contacted before. In this way once someone has contacted, say, the Microsoft Web server for the first time the ISP server will store the relevant IP address for future use.

If our ISP server does not know the relevant IP address it will contact one of the DNS servers that it has been programmed to look at and ask for the IP address using the same methods that we discussed earlier.

Once this IP address is known, contact is made between our client machine and the Web server; a communication takes place and the default page is downloaded to our client machine.

Why the default page? Quite simply because we have not specified a particular page just the Web server and almost all of them are now set up so that a default page will be provided should a user fail to specify a particular file.

The communication process is not permanently established. The connection is made and the first block of data is downloaded. The connection is then broken to allow others to access the server and after a while our client re-establishes a connection and another section is downloaded and so on.

Depending on the quantity of data downloaded and the number of users connected to the server at any given time this process could be very erratic and the connection with the server could be broken at any time.

The whole process is controlled by a series of timers all intended to "smooth out" the connections on a less busy network. These timers are written into the software and occur at the client and server ends of the connection.

This method worked very well in the early days of the Web; however, with today's pressures – a large number of users and a huge volume of data – it is becoming less and less efficient.

There are plans afoot for changes to the way in which the HTTP protocol works in order to make it more suited for current uses. Many of these changes will be implemented during the next couple of years but the average user will be unaware of any fundamental difference in how the two systems work.

In addition to the explosive growth in the number of Web pages their content has also become much more complex, thus placing ever-greater demands on the Internet's infrastructure. With the insatiable demand to produce increasingly "fancy" pages with "clever features" server producers have asked for ways in which servers can download either small programs or specific data to the client computers – usually without the knowledge of the clients.

Originally this data was in the form of lines of text (called cookies) which would be downloaded to the client computer so that when the server was next contacted it would have some prearranged information already set up on the client machine. The overall aim of this was to provide a "faster" response time for the initial connection.

An extension of this idea produced the evolution of a number of specialised programming languages or, more correctly, programming interfaces onto the Web pages. Three of these are called Java, JavaScript and Active Server Pages (ASP). Java was developed by SUN computers, JavaScript by Netscape and ASP by Microsoft. This is typical of the development process when a new technology evolves. A number of companies compete with their version of "the solution"; eventually, one of them predominates and the others gradually vanish.

The various systems do roughly the same thing. They allow the server to download a program from itself to the client machine and then have this little program run on the client's computer. In theory it allows the system to produce simple "moving graphics" or interactive "question and answer" dialogs and in practice it does all of these things. The pages are "brighter" and far more interactive than they used to be but at a performance cost. Quite simply the sheer quantity of data that is moved around the Internet by these systems is part of the problem of poor performance and poor response-times which sometimes affect us.

Should you use the Web and the Web technologies in your business? It is certainly the future trend in terms of allowing prospective customers to contact your organisation, place orders, look for information and see your organisation as a "modern, dynamic company". Consider the Web site and the associated Web pages as the new "shop window". By having a presence on the Internet people can be made aware of your company's activities and services, irrespective of whether your organisation has two or twenty thousand employees.

What about using the Web as a means of providing an internal message board? In this too the Web technologies are useful. A company can have a Web server where useful internal information is placed concerning events, product lists, price lists, employee information, timetables and so on. Any employee with a computer can access this server and see the information. Similarly, this information can be automatically updated from databases, spreadsheets and word processed documents to allow employees to search for either specific information or general inquiries. All of this is available at considerably lower costs than the equivalent paper-based systems.

Security is an issue. The Web server needs to be set up properly so that sensitive documents or data can only be accessed by the correct users. This is doubly so if your Web server can be accessed from the Internet. A specific discussion of security issues is outside the scope of this book. Some general issues will be discussed in a later chapter.

Chapter 7

Electronic Mail (e-mail)

Instant Communication?

Electronic mail was one of the main reasons for the rapid growth of the Internet. The ability to send messages in text format all over the world has its appeal to the business community, the military establishment and academic centres. Once again, what no one appreciated was how rapidly this capability would be taken up and embraced by the computer community at large.

Since the concept of electronic mail (e-mail) was fundamental to the development of larger (wide area) networks – and to the Internet in general – it would be safe to assume that the original designs and methods have gone through considerable change and modification. This is definitely the case. The initial requirements and purposes of the e-mail community has been replaced by greater demands for visual enhancements, security, movies and sound. None of these were of concern to the original designers and so the systems themselves have gone through considerable modification – and continue to do so.

To understand some of the problems facing a modern installation of e-mail let us take a brief look at the early implementations.

One of the earliest forms of e-mail was found in the UNIX world. UNIX itself had started life as an operating system which was aimed at being able to provide remote control and communication services. In this situation one of the most important requirements was for users to be able to communicate with each other and exchange text-based information about system problems, technical reports and so on.

As might be expected, even in the early days a number of different solutions were developed with the specific aim of providing e-mail capability. We will not discuss these in detail here but concentrate on some of the more important e-mail systems that have developed over the years.

It must be stressed that e-mail is such an important part of the Internet that for many users it is the only aspect that they are interested in. Because of this there is continual development of the various e-mail systems aimed at giving the user greater capabilities and greater flexibility. We will be discussing the "standard" aspects of e-mail as much as that is possible. One of the earliest forms of e-mail was a utility called UUCP (UNIX-to-UNIX Copy Program) and it formed the basis for many early e-mail systems. In UUCP mail was sent from one machine to another in a series of hops.

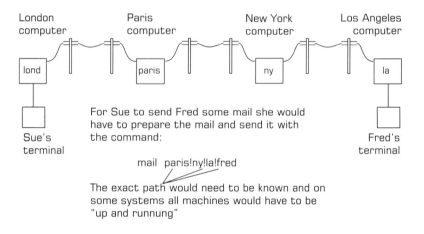

Figure 7.1   UUCP (UNIX-to-UNIX copy program) – old e-mail!

The local user would type something like abc!xyz!pqr!joec Here the recipient joec on machine pqr gets the data that is sent from a remote machine. In Figure 7.1 Sue would send mail to Fred by typing

```
mail paris!ny!la!fred
```

and then she would compose the message. The preceding command says "Send mail to Fred on the LA computer by way of New York and Paris".

This type of system was relatively complex to set-up. While it was quite capable of covering long distances the actual means of addressing machines and getting the data from the source computer (the one where the message originates) to the target computer (the one where the recipient resides) could be quite cumbersome.

Another approach was to have a system whereby a user could specify the target machine and the recipient's name. These two factors alone should be adequate for the e-mail message to get to the target machine. But would it? How could our sending computer be able to transmit the message to a machine whose whereabouts it does not know?

In comes our good old friend DNS. Let us say that we are sending a message to Fred who is a user at Sportsco's eastern sales computer. Fred's address would be something like this:[1]

```
fred@sales.east.sportsco.com
```

When we send the message our computer looks for the IP address of the sportsco machine. If this is not known then the DNS server is contacted and the usual DNS resolution process begins. Our machine eventually obtains the IP address of the sportsco computer and contacts it directly. The sportsco computer then informs Fred that some e-mail has arrived for him.

Flexible Mail

Here we see the way in which the Internet technologies have proved to be so successful. One of the tools (e-mail) cannot resolve addresses so it passes the task over to the tool that is specifically aimed at address resolution (DNS). This sorts out the address resolution and then hands the result back to the e-mail program which then continues.

The general program or protocol that provides this level of e-mail service is called SMTP (Simple Mail Transfer Protocol). In this, one side of the communication sends data to the recipient and has no responsibility for storing the messages. SMTP is very much a "send and forget" method of transferring messages. This type of mail delivery system is called end-to-end delivery.

Unlike the UUCP method this type of delivery does not rely on intermediate client computers. It is a significant improvement over UUCP but it has one major drawback. As standard, SMTP requires both the

---

1. The implied structure here does *not* directly relate to our earlier "Sportsco" examples.

sending and receiving system to be fully capable of handling mail. What this means is that both systems need to be switched on and running for it to work. This was the case when most machines on the Internet were large (almost mainframe) UNIX servers. They tended to be switched on and left running for long periods of time (often many months or years). With the growth and proliferation of PCs the machines were often switched off during the night and for frequent periods during the day. Clearly, SMTP would fail if this were the case.

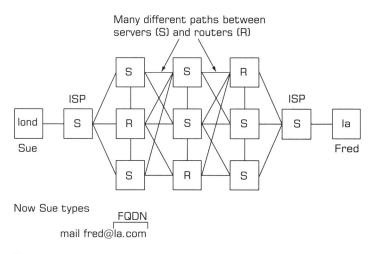

Figure 7.2   SMTP e-mail

A modification to the original SMTP specification allows the system to try delivery a number of times. These parameters are configurable by the system administrator and a common standard is that the system will try and deliver mail three times in the first couple of hours and then revert to a "once more in a week's time" type of approach. This is better but not good enough for the average PC user. These people are used to a more "forgiving" type of system.

Post Offices

What is required is the facility of having a central mail server that stores the incoming e-mail messages and then allows users to retrieve their mail at a time to suite themselves. This facility is provided by another Internet protocol called POP (Post Office Protocol). There are two common POP protocols that differ in their overall functionality. Their names are POP2 and POP3. Most modern systems use POP3, the later development, or its newer replacement IMAP (Internet Message Access Protocol). What does POP add to our e-mail capability? Quite simply the ability to store e-mail messages on a server and for us to contact the server and choose to download (or read) messages one at a time. Is this revolutionary? Now it seems rather "old hat" but when it appeared some ten years ago it was seen as a revolutionary technique.

Using one of the POP protocols a user can connect to a server and see what messages they have. They can then choose to read, make a copy (download) or delete these messages. Later additions to the POP standard have added additional functionality, stronger security and made a product more suited to today's user requirements.

In essence, a POP server acts as a repository of incoming e-mail messages. The user then contacts this repository and gains access to their messages. Depending on the security requirements of the server there may be more or less interrogation of the user to check their validity. Figure 7.3 illustrates the principle.

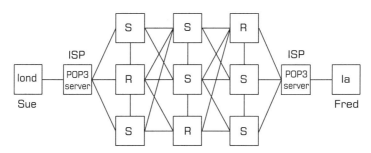

Now Sue mails Fred with

    mail fred@la.com

and since Fred's ISP server is POP3-compliant, it stores the message until Fred's machine is switched on and Fred contacts the server. He is then told "You have x messages waiting"

Figure 7.3 POP3 mail

Figure 7.4
Modern
e-mail
(Netscape
Navigator)

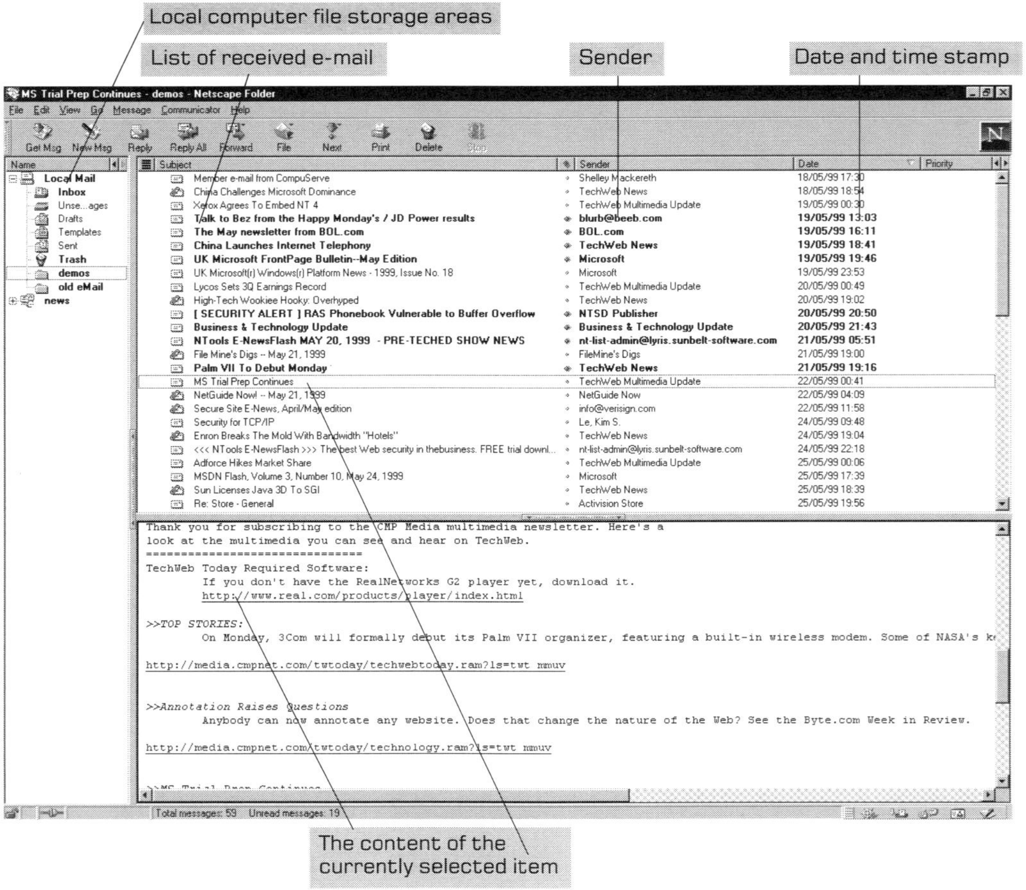

While the earlier (command-line) mail systems might be fine for UNIX "techies" most people would find the required dialogs very daunting. Modern systems use a "friendlier" graphical interface to connect to their mail servers. Figure 7.4 shows an example from Netscape Navigator.

The POP server approach added the type of functionality that most users wanted. They could now go to the server and access their mail any time they wanted. The addition of the various graphical interfaces meant that the whole system was considerably more useable by a wider audience.

The enhancements that POP gave to the whole e-mail system could not have anticipated the explosive growth in the Internet community. In the same way it could not anticipate the demands placed on the Internet by the desire to send not just text messages (as in the original plan) but documents laid out with additional fonts, graphic images, sound, movies and so on. An additional enhancement was necessary for this to work correctly.

This enhancement was another protocol called MIME (Multipurpose Internet Mail Extensions). In this protocol it was possible for users to attach a range of additional file types (formatted documents, sound clips, video, pictures and other graphics) to the basic e-mail system. We now have the basis of a modern e-mail system running on top of our TCP/IP communications programs. Figure 7.5 illustrates how a corporate e-mail system might work.

E-mail continues to be one of the major components of Internet activity. You can expect continual enhancement and additional features in all mail systems as vendors try to give their products "competitive edge".

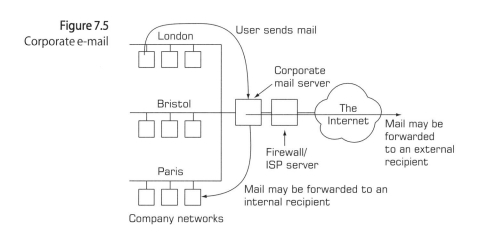

Figure 7.5
Corporate e-mail

London

User sends mail

Corporate mail server

Bristol

The Internet

Mail may be forwarded to an external recipient

Firewall/ ISP server

Paris

Mail may be forwarded to an internal recipient

Company networks

Chapter 8

DHCP (Dynamic Host Configuration Protocol)

Automatic Configuration

So far we have seen that it is necessary to set up and configure our computers to use an IP address, a subnet mask and various other components. These components are programs (protocols) like DNS, WINS and some other aspects that are outside the scope of this book. What if we do not want to have to do this each time that another computer is added onto our system or, alternatively, perhaps we have a salesforce that travels round the countryside going into each of our main offices to submit quotes, check price lists and so on. In each of these cases they will need to connect to the local office network. Should we expect them to configure the IP component of their computer each time they log onto the network? The answer is almost certainly no. In situations like this DHCP (Dynamic Host Configuration Protocol) is the solution.

DHCP is, surprise, surprise, a development of an earlier protocol called BOOTP (Boot Protocol). BOOTP was intended to be used by diskless workstations (computers without a hard disk drive) that would use BOOTP to connect to a main server and get all the necessary startup programs off of that. BOOTP is still in use in some situations since it is useful for automatic downloading of programs and data, but it is now steadily being replaced by DHCP.

A DHCP server is set up to contain a pool of valid IP addresses. These, together with the relevant subnet mask and whatever other information is required, are allocated to a computer as the client machine attaches to the network.

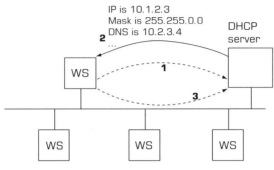

IP is 10.1.2.3
Mask is 255.255.0.0
DNS is 10.2.3.4

DHCP server — This is configured to have all the network information that the clients will require. This includes IP address, the address of the DNS server, WINS server, routers and so on. There are many different parameters that can be configured

1 When the workstation first starts up it contacts the DHCP server and requests its setup information

2 The DHCP server will usually grant this information together with a lease (period of time for which this information is valid)

3 50% of the way through the lease the client contacts the DHCP server and requests lease renewal. This is usually granted

Figure 8.1   DHCP

The DHCP server can be used to allocate this information on a permanent basis or on a leasehold basis. This latter use is relevant to our "travelling salesman" example. Let us use a modification to our earlier, Sportsco, example as an illustration. Imagine that we have set up regional offices called East, West and South. A salesman arrives at the East office to upload (transfer) some orders to the main server. These orders would then become part of the standard "ordering" system within the company. Before this, of course, the salesman must get onto the network.

The DHCP server in the East office offers our salesman's computer all of the relevant IP setup data but for a limited time of, say, one hour. After this if the salesman is no longer working on the system the DHCP server will reclaim the IP address and re-allocate it to the address pool.

When the salesman travels round the country and visits the North office the same process is repeated and he or she is allocated an IP address relevant to that site.

In the above example, the IP addresses are allocated for a finite period only. If an address is required for a longer period the salesman's computer will "renegotiate" with the server for a lease extension. In most cases this would be granted and the salesman allowed to continue with the connection. When they eventually disconnect, the system will reclaim the IP address and return it to the relevant pool of IP addresses.

DHCP allows for the automatic allocation of IP addresses either for a limited period of time (leases) or as a permanent allocation. The sensible integration of DHCP into a network can simplify the allocation and setup of IP addresses and assist in the configuration of DNS and WINS servers.

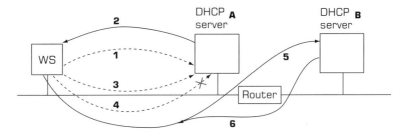

1 The client workstation requests information
2 This is granted by the server for a lease period
   (say 10 days)
3 After 50% of the lease period (5 days in our example)
   the client requests lease renewal. This will usually be
   granted unless the server is very busy. If the server
   is busy, the client waits until 7/8 of the lease has expired
4 After this time, if the server still fails to renew the lease...
5 The client tries any other servers on the network. It could
   actually apply to the original server for a new lease
6 If one of the remote DHCP servers grants a lease the whole
   process starts again with a new lease renegotiation after
   50% of the lease period

Figure 8.2   DHCP renegotiation (simplified)

Use of DHCP raises some security issues in connection with "automatic" connection of people to the organisation's network. This is not a concern in some networks. If security is an issue then consult a security professional to discuss these matters in more depth.

Chapter 9

Index Server and Proxy Server

These two products are relatively recent additions to Microsoft's stable of Internet services. A number of software vendors produce proxy servers but currently Microsoft's Index Server is the only "standard issue" indexing tool available. These two products are complimentary additions to the Microsoft range of Internet tools. They help you to build a powerful, controlled and adaptable corporate Intranet system.

Index Server

Have you ever been in a situation where you need a letter or document but you cannot find it on your computer? This is bad enough with a small home computer but when it is your company's computer with many tens of thousands of documents the task becomes even more daunting.

Index Server solves this type of problem. Firstly, it is a document indexing system which, once the indexes have been built up, can dynamically update the indexes as new material is added. You can select one directory or a whole drive to index – of course, the indexing process takes proportionately longer the larger the drive. For a drive containing a couple of hundred thousand documents the initial indexing process could take as long as 24 hours to complete. This is, of course, very machine-dependant.

Once the index has been built up Microsoft produce a search tool (called a search engine) which takes your requests and searches the index for documents that match your requirements. If your search is a simple one and you have a large number of documents the results (a large number of document references) will be displayed in your browser once the search completes. By making the search criteria more specific you can select a more specific range of documents.

All of the searching and selection (and in fact the initial indexing procedures) are all handled through Web browser interfaces. This is becoming the standard method of accepting and presenting information to users.

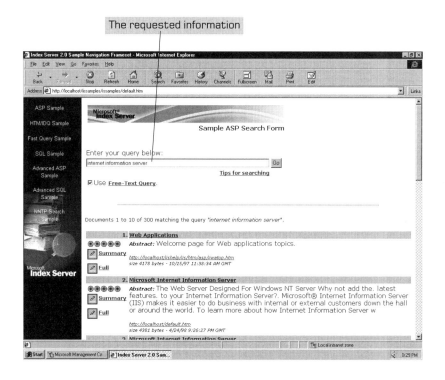

Figure 9.1 Sample Index Server screen – request and output

In the sample screen above you will see that the requested information is internet information server. This is entered into the "Enter your query below:" box. By pressing the "Go" button the system searches the server and produces a list of files that match the search criteria.

In our example we had some 2500 documents running on a server with a Pentium 233 Mhz processor and 128 Mb of memory. The whole indexing procedure took less than three minutes and the search took place almost instantaneously. These timings would change considerably with a much larger number of documents.

In addition to simple searches Index Server can support a complex series of "structured questions" with these you can search for word combinations so that a search could stipulate that you wanted the word "sales" within three words of "1998" and so on.

When it finds matches Index Server produces a summary of the document. You are then presented with two options on the left-hand side of each document. These options are to view either the full document or an abstract of the document. In this way you are able to check through a list documents without having to open each and every one.

Index Server produces groups of documents that match the search criteria. If there are too many documents to be displayed all at once, the server displays them in batches (depending on the size of the text in the actual documents). In this way you can start with a general search and then refine the search to make the list of documents more suitable to your purposes.

Index Server is an additional component to the Microsoft Web server (Internet Information Server). It is provided free of charge by Microsoft and represents the best way to index and search through large volumes of documents. All searching and the output from the searches are done through the Web browser. If you can use a browser you can use Index Server either on your local machine or remotely across the Internet. In this way you could be at home and search the "electronic filing cabinet" from the comfort of your home office.

Proxy Server

Many companies are interested in providing their staff with limited Internet access but are concerned with how they can control indiscreet or improper use of this valuable resource. They would like to restrict the sites visited and possibly the times of day in which the Internet can be contacted. They would also like to provide a degree of security to protect their internal network from the outside world.

Microsoft's Proxy Server is a product which provides businesses with these three important features:

- the ability to provide Internet access for their staff;

- control of their staff's access to the Internet;
- considerable protection to the internal network from the outside world.

How does it work?

To understand this let's look at a simple network design (Figure 9.2).

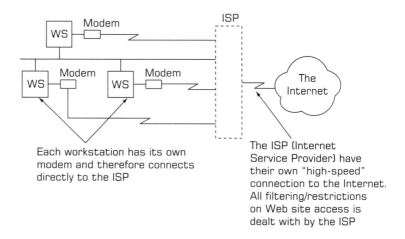

Each workstation has its own modem and therefore connects directly to the ISP

The ISP (Internet Service Provider) have their own "high-speed" connection to the Internet. All filtering/restrictions on Web site access is dealt with by the ISP

Figure 9.2 The older-style corporate Internet connection

In this design each of our users has to have their own IP address and network connection. This proves to be an expensive solution to the requirements of providing Internet connectivity. One approach is to use some modem-sharing software and to route all of our users' calls through this software. Although this provides a solution it does not give us the control that we wanted nor does it protect our internal network from any outside "attack". Once our computers are connected to the Internet then, in principle, any outside user could access our machines – particularly if we had been casual about setting up out network security. This chance of outside users seeing into our internal network is too great a risk for most companies and so they compromise the degree to which they provide Internet access. Let us look at the proxy server solution.

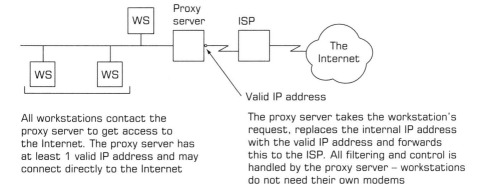

All workstations contact the proxy server to get access to the Internet. The proxy server has at least 1 valid IP address and may connect directly to the Internet

The proxy server takes the workstation's request, replaces the internal IP address with the valid IP address and forwards this to the ISP. All filtering and control is handled by the proxy server – workstations do not need their own modems

Figure 9.3   Corporate connection using a proxy server installation

Figure 9.4
More complex
proxy server

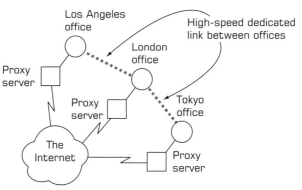

1   Each office connects through its own proxy server

2   All filtering and control is applied at each proxy server

3   When the local Internet connection of one office is busy, traffic can be rerouted to the quieter office and from there out onto the Internet. So when London is busy, but it is nightime in Los Angeles (LA), traffic is sent through the dedicated high-speed link from London to LA and then out onto the quieter Internet connections in LA. In this way, optimal Internet connectivity can be maintained

Here our internal network accesses the Internet through the proxy server. At the "Internet" end of the connection the proxy server has a valid IP address. This address is usually assigned by the Internet Service

Provider and could mean that the IP address is our company's registered IP address. There is, of course, nothing to stop our company having more than one valid IP address.

Our internal network is quite separate from the external (Internet) network. Here we use one of the unassigned IP addresses. I prefer to use the 10.0.0.0 network address – this gives us all of the flexibility of a Class A address and allows for future expansion of our company.

How Does the Proxy Server Work?

Any of our users who wish to access an Internet site does so through the proxy server. Let us look at an example.

Say user Fred on machine 10.4.3.2 wants to contact the site `www.microsoft.com` and that our proxy server has a valid IP address of 155.155.144.1 (this IP address is used as an illustration).

Fred's machine is initially set up to direct all requests to the proxy server. The proxy server intercepts this request and processes it so that to the outside world it looks as though the request has come from the valid IP address of 153.155.144.1.

After this the DNS lookup and all other stages continue as normal. When the data comes back from `www.microsoft.com` the reverse process occurs. The proxy server – which has kept a record of which machine the data originally came from – intercepts the incoming data, readdresses it and sends it back onto the internal network to the original user.

All that the original user is aware of is a slight "delay" in the processing of the original data. The entire process is effectively hidden from the user.

If this was all that Proxy Server provided it would be adequate for most purposes. With the above capabilities users could access the Internet without having to have multiple modems or multiple ISP (Internet Service Providers) accounts. Equally, other users or organisations on the Internet could not gain access to our network through the proxy server. It provides us with a reasonable degree of security and a simpler means of connecting to the Internet.

In addition, our proxy server allows caching and filtering of the users who are accessing the Internet through it. What exactly do we mean by caching, in this context?

When a user contacts an Internet site for the first time and downloads a couple of Web pages from the site, our proxy server will store these pages on its own hard disk. If another user some time after the first wants to contact the same Internet site and wishes to download the same Web pages these pages will be delivered from the locally cached (copied) versions. In other words, our local server will deliver the data instead of the data coming from the Internet. This means two things:

1. The local user sees a much faster response from the local server than if the data had come from the Internet;
2. The Internet connection carries less data and so the cost of the Internet connection should be reduced as a result.

Additional Benefits

So far so good but there is more. With the latest version of Proxy Server it is possible to set the server to automatically download certain Web sites or certain parts of Web sites. These can be stored on our local server for access by our staff. Using this technique our proxy server could contain a local copy of all of the sites that interest us and our local users will only access data held on our local server. The server could be set to do the downloads during the night and therefore remove the need for our users to contact the Internet during the working day. In this way the proxy server can give the appearance of Internet connectivity without running the risk of expensive connection charges and without users getting the temptation of browsing for hours on company time. All of this is quite separate from any e-mail access which can still function normally. The only limitation here is that modern Web sites use some additional programming functions (Active Server Pages and Java) which we mentioned earlier. These are not downloaded into the cache. Only the HTML component of the pages is currently copied onto the proxy server.

In systems where the above degree of isolation is seen as "too open" Proxy Server supplies a range of filters which allow an administrator to restrict the range of Web sites that a user can connect to and also the time at which a user can access the Internet. This, together with the ability to restrict bandwidth (so that one user cannot "hog" all of the available connections), means that it is possible to limit users according to their needs or their abilities.

Once connected to the Internet, using whichever method is preferred, Proxy Server blocks all attempts from users on the Internet to access the internal network. In this way the internal (company) network is relatively secure from unwanted access by external users.

Proxy Server is one of the most powerful pieces of software for corporate control and management of Internet access. When deployed in a sensible structured way it provides a company with access to the Internet with few of the "nightmare scenarios" that most companies are worried about. Proxy servers are set to become one of the corporate organisation's "standard" tools over the next few years. Although we have referred to Microsoft's product in this chapter there are many other excellent proxy servers in the marketplace, all of which provide essentially the same features as those discussed above.

Other Proxy Servers

One of the most established is Wingate at

```
http://wingate.deerfield.com
```

This is available in three versions covering small (home), medium and large networks. Visit the Web site for more details. It provides all of the features described above. It is reasonably priced and compares favourably with Microsoft's product. Other proxy servers exist – such as *Gauntlet* from Network Associates (www.nai.com). A little research on your part may find a cheaper alternative to those described above.

Chapter 10

SNMP (Simple Network Management Protocol)

The Need for Network Management

SNMP is one of the standard tools provided for administrators of Internet-based networks. It provides the framework for administrators to check, interrogate and modify settings on a computer network.

Essentially, the network is viewed as a series of "agents" that report events to a central management console. These "agents" can be computers, printers, routers or any of the other pieces of hardware that make up a networked system.

One of the problems with SNMP is that the original specification allowed for considerable "vendor modification" of the data being transferred. As such it is important to ensure that the management software and the various agents scattered around the network all understand the same "dialect" of SNMP. If this is done the only other issue is that some SNMP systems can generate a considerable amount of network "traffic" in their own right. On some systems this additional network traffic can be considered excessive and so only critical components of the network will be set up as SNMP agents and report events to the management system.

Under "perfect" conditions all processing components on a network could act as SNMP agents. By processing components I mean units which actually process the data (computers, printers, routers, bridges and so on) rather than the passive components (cables, wires, power supplies and so on). Ideally, the manager would require a suitable management machine with which to interrogate and analyse the network. This is usually done by means of a computer running suitable software.

SNMP has two major shortcomings:

1. The original standard was based on a command-line interface which can, at best, be described as clumsy. The only real way in which to make the system work is to use a graphical user interface. These tend to be proprietary and an interface produced by "Bloggs Computers" is unlikely to work completely with hardware from "Grummitt Computers".

2. The standard allowed for a variety of "vendor-dependent" modifications to be added. These further increased the differences between various vendor's offerings. In general, for SNMP to work an organisation should standardise on one management and agent product from one of the major manufacturers.

If the above problems are addressed then SNMP can be a good way of managing an internal network. Provided that the management system does not produce so much network traffic that it severely limits the overall network functionality, SNMP can be a powerful network management tool. The system itself works by a series of relatively simple commands like GET and PUT to either obtain data about a machine or to set a value into a machine. In this way a manager could find out how long a particular server had been up and running or what the percentage network throughput was on a particular network segment.

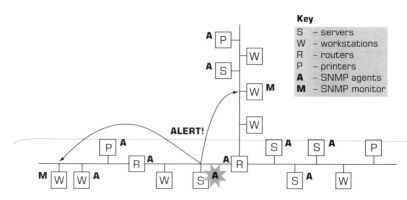

Here, the agents (usually important network or system components) report information back to the designated management consols (the SNMP monitors)
In the event of a major network malfunction a special alert can be sent to the various monitors thus informing them of the problem

Figure 10.1 SNMP – network management

Most modern SNMP systems allow the user to collate and report on a variety of network situations. In this way SNMP can be used to report whenever the overall network utilisation is, say, above 75%. This type of objective data is essential for accurate management and correct decision-making.

In the previous diagram the alerts referred to can be any unusual network event, excess traffic, a machine failing etc. These alerts can be programmed to e-mail an administrator, or to draw their attention to the event in some agreed way. By using this method, potentially disastrous network situations can usually be avoided, or their effects minimised.

Chapter 11

Security, Secrets and Electronic Commerce (e-commerce)

The Need for Security

In this chapter we cover a number of complex but important topics. The specialists will cry out in horror at some of the simplifications that I make here. My only excuse is that I want to convey the general *principles* covering how these technologies work rather than immersing myself in detailed discussions of each of the systems themselves.

So far we have talked about the various technologies that comprise the "typical" intranet or Internet set-up. These have included FTP, WWW, e-mail and a number of others. One of the biggest growth areas over the next few years is going to be electronic commerce (e-commerce). Many different organisations are looking into the prospects and potential benefits of running some form of e-business. These companies range from the multinational airlines running ticket booking services through to small independent staff agencies and local high-street grocery stores who are offering electronic shopping with home delivery services. Whichever way you look at it the world of commerce and shopping for goods and services will never be the same.

What benefits do these electronic services offer? Quite simply it is cost savings and the opportunity of reaching a far wider audience than would otherwise be available. It can cost relatively little money to set up a sophisticated Web site which corresponds to a high street shop. This can be promoted world-wide via the Web to reach an audience of many tens of millions of people. When orders are placed on the Web server they can be written into a database, the orders dispatched and the warehouse restocked. If the database has been written correctly the system can send out update messages to the client telling them when the goods have been dispatched and the status of the order. All of this can be done remotely without the client knowing exactly where the goods have been shipped from or the actual location of the warehouse. If a new "corporate image" is required it takes a few days to organise and re-present the corporate Web site. This has to be compared with the many months that it would take for the same process to be done using bricks and mortar.

With any such system one of the major obstacles is to gain customer acceptance of what is a new and in many cases daunting technology. One of the major concerns is the security of such systems.

When the Internet was in its infancy the only people who were using it were military personnel or academic staff involved in the design of the basic system. As such, all of these people were "trusted" and so the whole Internet community was made up from individuals who posed no threat to the system as a whole. If you were not trusted you simply were not allowed onto the system.

The Internet has, in many ways, become a victim of its own success. The Internet community now comprises many millions of people world-wide and as in any large community there are the "good-guys" and the "bad-guys". So what are the problems?

Put simply, all commands and data sent through the Internet (in the standard form) is sent "in the clear". This means that any person equipped with the correct piece of software can "listen in" to an Internet or intranet exchange and capture the information flowing between two computers. On the Internet this is no simple feat since there are many millions of users and the chance of "eavesdropping" on any given conversation is quite small. Needless to say most of us do not want our e-mail, Web sessions or any other information captured and intercepted by third parties, whoever they may be.

The following sequence of screenshots (Figures 11.1 to 11.10) show some analysis of a simple FTP session. In the lower pane of each screenshot you can see the data being transferred in its clear text form. This is the actual data travelling from the server to the client computer. Under some circumstances this could be very compromising! In general, the same principle applies to all data transferred over a "standard" TCP/IP connection. This data was collected using a standard network analyser or "sniffer". This type of software is provided as standard on many computer systems and can be freely downloaded from the Internet.

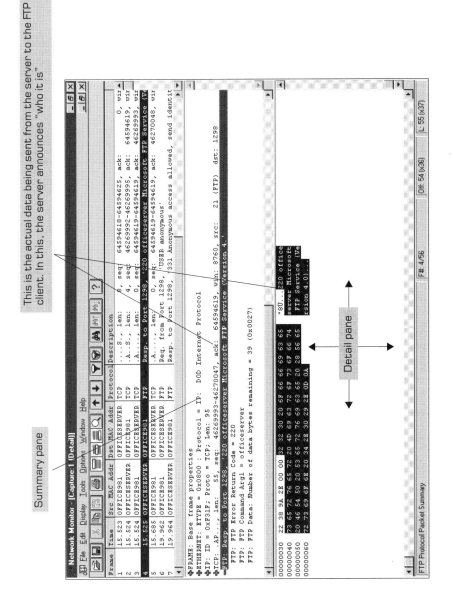

Figure 11.1　TCP data analysis (1)

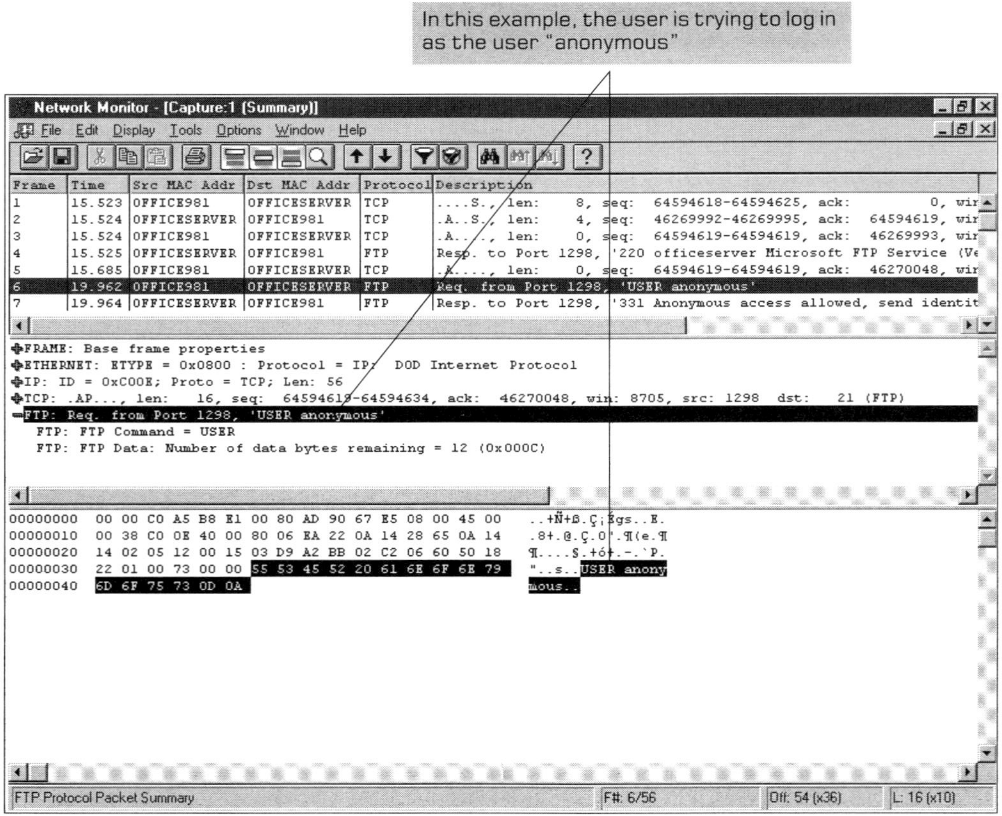

Figure 11.2 TCP data analysis (2)

The server replies that it will accept an anonymous user. It requests that the user enters their e-mail address as a password.

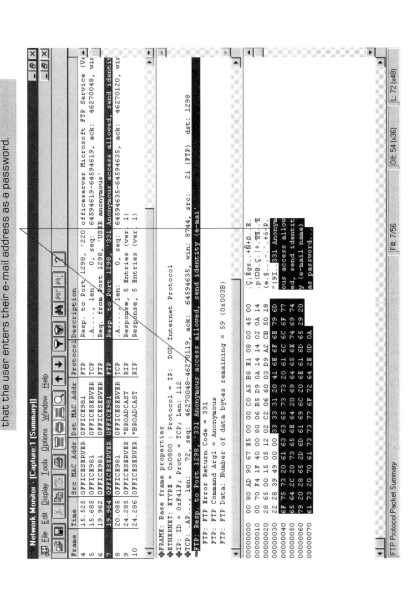

Figure 11.3   TCP data analysis (3)

The user responds with their e-mail address:
ks@work.com

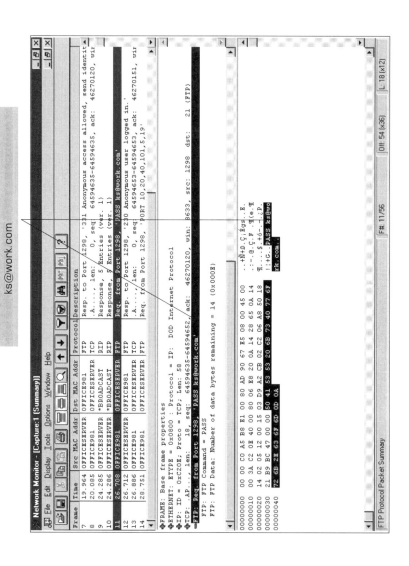

Figure 11.4   TCP data analysis (4)

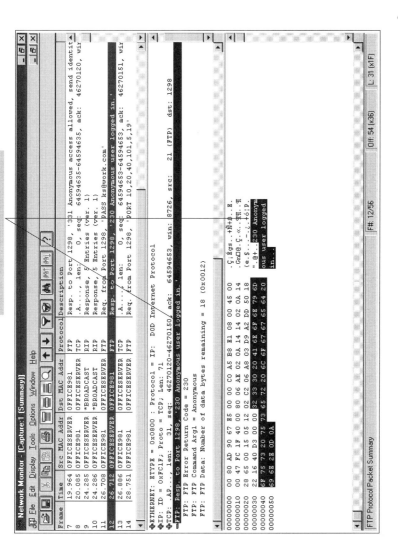

Figure 11.5 TCP data analysis (5)

The client has requested a list of the files that the server has.
The server replies with the name of its 1 file (this is only an illustration). The file is called "secret.txt"

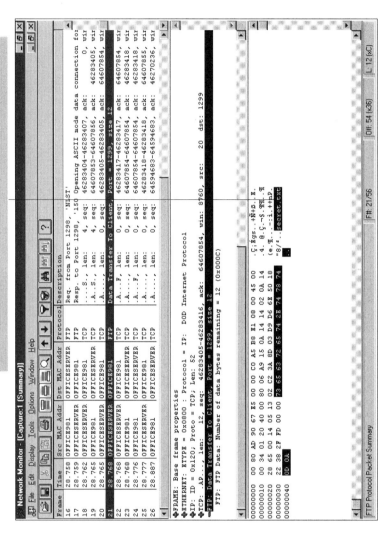

Figure 11.6   TCP data analysis (6)

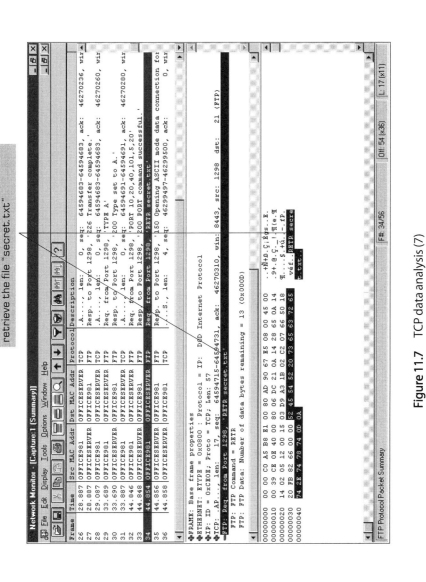

Figure 11.7 TCP data analysis (7)

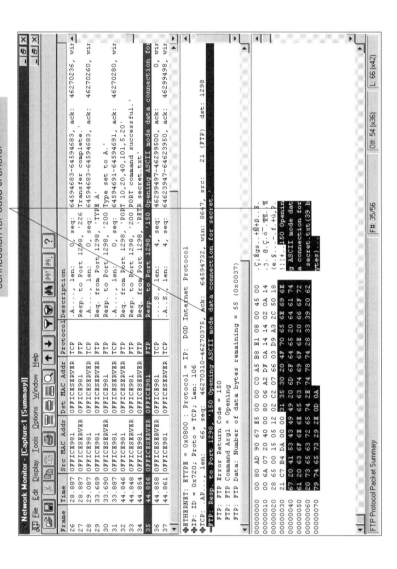

Figure 11.8 TCP data analysis (8)

Here we see the file transfer in place – including the contents of the file!

Network Monitor - [Capture:1 (Summary)]

File Edit Display Tools Options Window Help

Frame	Time	Src MAC Addr	Dst MAC Addr	Protocol	Description
33	44.848	OFFICESERVER	OFFICE981	FTP	Resp. to Port 1298, '200 PORT command successful.'
34	44.854	OFFICE981	OFFICESERVER	FTP	Req. from Port 1298, 'RETR secret.txt'
35	44.856	OFFICESERVER	OFFICE981	FTP	Resp. to Port 1298, '150 Opening ASCII mode data connection for
36	44.858	OFFICE981	OFFICESERVER	TCP	....S., len: 4, seq: 46299497-46299500, ack: 0, wir
37	44.861	OFFICESERVER	OFFICE981	TCP	.A..S., len: 4, seq: 64623947-64623950, ack: 46299498, wir
38	44.861	OFFICE981	OFFICESERVER	TCP	.A....., len: 0, seq: 46299498-46299498, ack: 64623948, wir
39	44.863	OFFICESERVER	OFFICE981	FTP	Data Transfer To Client, Port = 1300, size 39
40	44.989	OFFICE981	OFFICESERVER	TCP	.A....., len: 0, seq: 64623948-64623948, ack: 46299537, wir
41	44.989	OFFICE981	OFFICESERVER	TCP	.A....., len: 0, seq: 64594732-64594732, ack: 46270376, wir
42	44.990	OFFICESERVER	OFFICE981	TCP	.A....F., len: 0, seq: 46299537-46299537, ack: 64623948, wir
43	44.990	OFFICE981	OFFICESERVER	TCP	.A....., len: 0, seq: 64623948-64623948, ack: 46299538, wir
44	44.990	OFFICESERVER	OFFICE981	FTP	Resp. to Port 1298, '226 Transfer complete.'

FRAME: Base frame properties
ETHERNET: ETYPE = 0x0800 : Protocol = IP: DOD Internet Protocol
IP: ID = 0xA20; Proto = TCP; Len: 79
TCP: .AP...., len: 39, seq: 46299498-46299536, ack: 64623948, win: 8760, src: 20 dst: 1300
  FTP: FTP Data Transfer To Client, Port = 1300, size 39
    FTP: FTP Data: Number of data bytes remaining = 39 (0x0027)

```
00000000  00 80 AD 90 67 E5 00 00  C0 A5 B8 E1 08 00 45 00   .Çı Ågs. +Ñ+B. E.
00000010  00 4F 0A 20 40 00 80 06  9F FA 0A 14 14 02 0A 14   .O . @.Ç.ƒ. ÿÑ¦.¶
00000020  28 65 00 14 05 14 02 C2  79 6A 03 DA 15 4C 50 18   (e.¶.¶.-yj.+SLP.
00000030  22 38 15 09 00 00 48 65  6C 6C 6F 20 74 68 69 73   "8§....Hello this
00000040  20 69 73 20 73 65 63 72  65 74 20 20 0D 0A 0D 0A    is secret    ....
00000050  0A 0D 0A 4F 4B 4B 0D 0A  0D 0A 0D 0A 0D 0A 0A      ...OKK........
```

FTP Protocol Packet Summary   F#: 39/56   Off: 54 (x36)   L: 39 (x27)

Figure 11.9   TCP data analysis (9)

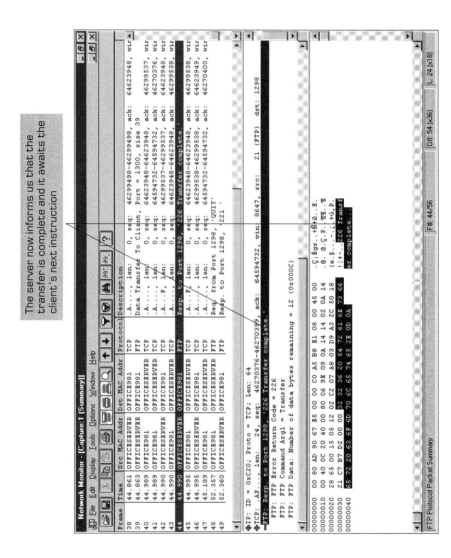

Figure 11.10 TCP data analysis (10)

As you can see from the previous screenshots, all text/passwords/data is sent "in the clear" across TCP/IP. What can be done about this? How can we protect our data and guarantee our client's authenticity? How can we prove who we are to our clients?

Protecting our Data

The answer to all of these questions takes us into the "murky" world of encryption and computer security. First of all let us clarify what we mean by encryption.

In essence, this is the process whereby we can hide our data from prying eyes. Most systems use a means of securing the data that can be divided into two parts. These are the algorithm (process) and the key. Algorithms are the techniques used to conceal the patterns of data in a message. The *keys* are patterns of binary digits that are fed into the algorithm together with the data to produce an unreadable and indecipherable output. This output is often referred to as *cyphertext*.

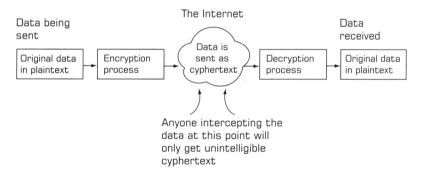

Figure 11.11   Encryption basics

Modern algorithms are very complex and, ideally, they are publicly available. Why should this be? The answer is that most specialists working in the encryption industry feel that an algorithm which is publicly understood and, as such, has not been found to have any flaws is a far more reliable system than a secret one. A "secret algorithm" – which is thought to be secure – will not have been subjected to public scrutiny and might actually be so flawed that it is useless. Often in the encryption world a supposedly secure system is found to be easily broken and rapidly falls out of use. An ideal encryption system is one which uses a universally recognised algorithm that has been found to be "unbreakable" as long as the key is suitably long. Why is the role of the key so important? To illustrate this let us look at one of the oldest forms of encryption. This is called the *Caesar cipher*. In this the position of each letter in the alphabet is moved a number of places and transposed with the corresponding letter. With a move of 2 the letter A becomes C, the letter G becomes I and so on. In this way the word HELLO becomes JGNNQ. And any phrase or sentence transposed in this way becomes quite unreadable to the untrained eye.

With a more sophisticated method of encryption, the above (simple) methods of transposition could be made far more difficult to break. If we were able to change the process each time we applied the algorithm, the encrypted data would be more difficult to "crack". This in essence is the role of the key. It allows the person encrypting their data to have some degree of control over the complexity of the encryption process and by that fact to be able to make the whole encryption process more secure.

Clearly, such a simple system as the one above is easily broken. Part of the reason for the success of this system two thousand years ago was that the majority of the population – through which the message passed – were illiterate, thus considerably adding to the security of the system!

A modern algorithm uses many far more complex stages in its adjustment of the message. The key, an integral part of the whole encryption process, should add further confidentiality to this whole process. The size and complexity of the key should have a direct relationship with how easy (or difficult) it is, given the output, to work out what the original text should be.

A key of two bits in length gives us only four ways of affecting the algorithm. We could "feed in" to our algorithm the patterns 00, 01, 10, 11 any of which would produce a different cyphertext. Anyone trying to break our code would only have to work out the algorithm (not difficult to do with an open algorithm!) and then try the different bit patterns from the key. With a two-bit key this means four combinations – not too difficult to do even by hand!

A three-bit key gives us eight possibilities (000, 001, 010, 011, 100, 101, 110, 111). Again each of these patterns would produce a different form of cyphertext. By the time we have a 40-bit key (the commonest default for most systems) we have 1,099,511,627,776 possibilities. Each one of these would have to be explored by someone trying to break our code. They could, of course, strike lucky and get the right number first time by chance, but this is unlikely. To a modern computer the above large number is not too difficult to break and can be done in a matter of hours or days, depending on the power of the machine.

So, to secure your data would you feel happier with a 2-bit key, a 3-bit key or a 40-bit key. The answer is, of course, the 40-bit key. If you wanted much greater security would 40 bits be strong enough? Unfortunately not. Modern software can produce key lengths of over 4000 bits. The price that is paid for this greater security is that the computer becomes much slower as it has to process all of the data during the encryption process. In general the longer the key length the more secure the data.

One of the most important aspects of this whole process is the question "how secure must your data be". For a business involved in trading stock prices the security of their information may only be essential for a couple of hours. After that time the information is freely available and additional security would be deemed unnecessary. For a government involved in military planning over a 25-year period the security requirements would demand a system that could be secure for all of this time. The key length would then have to be very long and the algorithm would almost certainly remain secret.

Key length	Power of 2	Possibilities
2	2^2	4
3	2^3	8
16	2^{16}	65,536
30	2^{30}	1,073,741,824
40	$(*)2^{40}$	1,099,511,627,776
128	$(**)2^{128}$	340,282,366,920,938,463,463, 374,607,431,768,211,456

(*) Most standard security on computers works on this length of key. On most systems this could be "broken" by a brute-force attack in a matter of hours (days on older computers)
(**) Generally considered "secure" for most purposes (non-military)

Figure 11.12   The relationship between key length and "crackability"

Nowadays 40-bit keys are considered very minimal security. 128-bit keys are considered "secure" for most general purposes and longer key lengths take us into the "very secure" or military areas.

As an example most of us use a 4-digit "PIN" for our credit/cash cards. This number corresponds to a 32-bit key (eight bits for each digit). This would be seen as "insecure" since the encrypted data could be translated to its original form in a matter of a few tens of minutes (on most modern computer systems). It is acceptable for general bank transactions since most of us are at the cash machine carrying out the transaction for a few seconds at most.

Virtual Private Networks

One of the earliest manifestations of encryption to find its way into corporate networks was the Virtual Private Network. In this, some software (or a hardware device) was placed in the network and this encrypted any of the data flowing between the different sites. As such, the secrecy of any data passing between the sites could be guaranteed. This guarantee is for as long as the keys are calculated as being "unbreakable". Microsoft ships a system called PPTP (Point to Point Tunnelling Protocol) with NT server. This allows companies to set up VPNs based on the 40-bit encryption software. If more security than this is required it is necessary to implement a third-party encryption product.

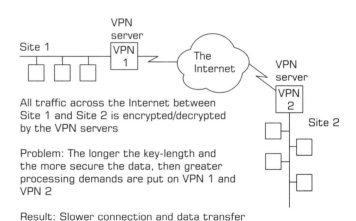

Figure 11.13   Virtual Private Networks

In such a VPN set-up the keys used to encrypt and decrypt the data are the same. This is referred to as *symmetric key encryption*. In this the same key is used to both conceal and to reveal the data. It is essential that the two sides of the data exchange are aware of the keys and are certain that no third-party has had access to the keys and can therefore compromise the data exchange. Key management in such a set-up is an essential aspect of the overall security of the system.

As good as such a system is it does not allow us to authenticate a client coming into our network. Nor does it allow us to authenticate our system to an outside client. This is no good for electronic commerce even though it allows us to be confident in the security of the data flowing between the various aspects of our internal organisation.

Public–Private Keys

If we want to authenticate our clients, and we want to be able to prove our existence to prospective customers, then a more flexible and elegant solution is required.

The answer to this is in *public key encryption* (often referred to as *asymmetric key encryption*).

To understand how this works and some of the additional benefits that it brings to any organisation planning to conduct some form of electronic commerce we have to extend our understanding of the encryption process.

In our previous diagram we used the binary key as an essential part of the data encryption process and the same key carried out the process of unscrambling or decrypting the data. Imagine that a mathematical process is available which produces two keys. These keys work in a special way. If one of the keys (it doesn't matter which one) is used to encrypt the data then the second key in the pair must be used to decrypt the data. The same key cannot be used for both actions. This is, in essence, how the public key system works. The mathematical process which produces this key pair is well documented and uses a number of standard arithmetic tricks to produce two large numbers which work in the way described as well as possessing the feature that one of the keys cannot be used to generate the other.

One key in the key-pair is stored locally (and referred to as the *private* key) the other is stored on a central server (and referred to as the *public* key). Imagine two Internet users: Jim and Sue. They want to send some confidential e-mail to each other. How can they do this? Figure 11.14 shows how this is done. This is good stuff. They can now send data back and forth without having to exchange keys. Each uses the public key of the other to encrypt the message and the recipient uses their corresponding private key to decrypt the message.

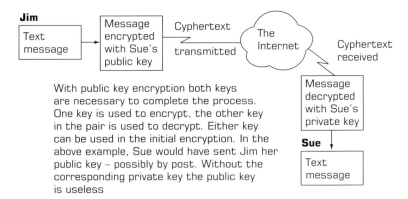

With public key encryption both keys are necessary to complete the process. One key is used to encrypt, the other key in the pair is used to decrypt. Either key can be used in the initial encryption. In the above example, Sue would have sent Jim her public key – possibly by post. Without the corresponding private key the public key is useless

Figure 11.14   Public and private keys

If it only did the above the system would be very useful. With a little more imagination the process can work some real miracles. Let us imagine that Jim's company wishes to place an order with Sue's company. Sue's company will not start to process the order unless they are confident that the order is genuine and that the client will not "pull out" of the deal at the last minute. In other words, they want to have confidence in the validity of the order. This can be done using the above system by adding in a process known as a *digital signature* to the encryption process. Figure 11.15 illustrates the principle.

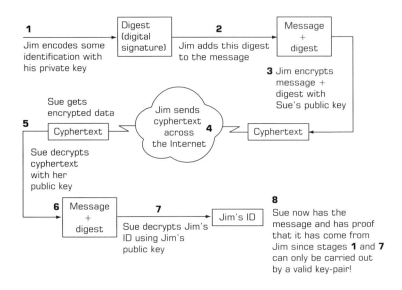

Figure 11.15   Digital signatures

All of this raises the question of who, exactly, will run the central server holding the public keys? The answer, quite simply, is that anyone can! This is perhaps a little too simplistic. Before we discuss this in more detail let us add some more "meat" to the discussion of digital signatures. If you wanted to secure your important financial database computers, but allow your senior staff to access them, you could employ a technique similar to the one described above. Instead of using just a simple private/public key system you would augment this with a more sophisticated form of identification – the *digital certificate*. This certificate would contain the user's private key, additional information about the person (department, internal phone number, tax reference and any other suitable data) and could be used by the client to identify themselves to the central server. Likewise, the central server could present its certificate so that clients would know they had connected to the correct part of the system. Once the two parts of the initial authentication had taken place the various keys could be used to encrypt/decrypt and sign the various messages and transfers. In such an arrangement the central server would be run and administered by the company's IT department. They would be responsible for the issuing of certificates, together with the public/private key pairs and also revoking the certificates as employees left the company or moved to a different part of the organisation. In this way the certificates and the associated public keys would be managed within the organisation. Microsoft and a number of other software companies provide software for doing just this.

A similar but less rigorous requirement could be found in a local club. Perhaps this club has decided to promote itself on the Internet. Its Web server has two parts to it: a general "public" area where anyone can visit and look at the pages, and a secure site that is only for club members. In this way general information about the club, its address, what it does, membership fees and so on can be made public while the minutes of the last meeting, forthcoming events, fund-raising discussions and so on could be kept only for members. When someone joins the club they are given a membership digital certificate that is used by the club server to authenticate them and allow them onto the secure site. Again, this could all be done by the club itself and they would be responsible for the issuing and management of the various certificates and, if required, the encryption keys.

A more rigorous approach would be required if we were opening a bank with an Internet facility. Clearly we would want to ensure that our customers were confident that they had connected to our organisation and also the bank would want to ensure that customers were themselves valid. This requirement is met by using a "trusted third party". In most cases the trusted party is a government agency or one of the major companies involved in this area. Currently, these certificates are issued by organisations such as Verisign, IBM, BT, Nortel and many others.

To summarise: our authenticating system could be in-house, or part of the organisation or could be provided by a centralised government agency. The best solution depends on how rigorous we want our authenticating system to be and whether we want the system to be publicly available.

Other Solutions

Most banks and other financial organisations use a combination of certification and an authenticating system called *challenge/response* to guarantee authentication. Once this has been done then a combination of public/private key encryption is used to protect the data. Figures 11.16 and 11.17 clarify the basic principles.

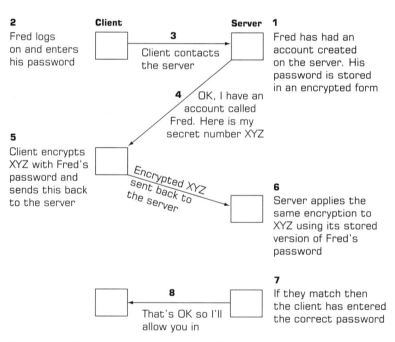

Figure 11.16   Challenge/response

In many cases the exact method of challenge/response is proprietary but most are based on the same general process. The most common form of certificate exchange uses a system called Secure Sockets Layer (SSL). This was developed by Netscape and is supported by most commonly available Web browsers in use today. The majority of companies doing business on the Internet use a combination of these systems in conjunction with the usual "password-based" means of authenticating users to form their integral Internet security system.

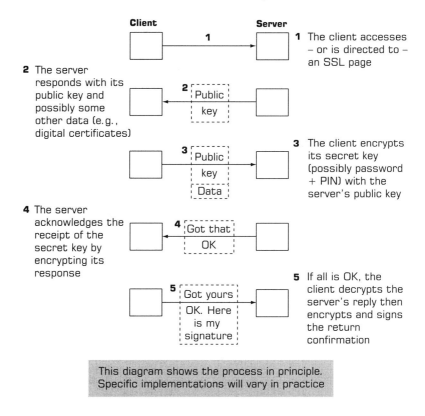

Figure 11.17   Secure sockets

In some instances the information required by the initial challenge response (the password and account reference) is sent by the bank or building society by post. As a separate mailing an additional PIN number (or something similar) is provided. Until all of these have been received the user is unable to contact the "secure" site. A combination of some, or all, of these methods is required to carry out any transactions. Some organisations use a two-tier system whereby customers can check balances and account details using passwords, digital-IDs and software certificates. They can only transfer money between accounts if they have all the above and a hardware ID (much like a credit card) that has to be used in a card-reader attached to the computer.

A complex implementation of SSL security with the associated public–private key exchanges is called SET (Secure Electronic Transaction). This involves the participation of banks, merchants, clients and certificating authorities, all of whom have to exchange and manage keys. In practice SET is proving to be very awkward to manage and implement and many organisations are accepting a theoretically less-secure but more workable solution. This "watered-down" SET still provides considerable security for the majority of transactions. The precise level of security needs to be set after a careful consideration of the company's specific requirements.

There are many different versions of the same basic principles found on most financial systems. The only common factor is that all digital and electronic security is set to increase steadily over the next few years as we all become absorbed into the rapid growth of the e-commerce world.

Chapter 12

Putting it all Together

We have now covered all of the components of a typical Internet or intranet system. Let us look at how these work together to give us a better understanding of how the whole system functions.

We will look at a number of different scenarios to assist us in our efforts. These may well exist as distinct entities and in some situations they will exist in combination to provide a more complex networking setup. Either way the following examples will clarify the points covered in the earlier chapters. In each of the following scenarios please remember that individual installations and networks will differ in specific layout and components. What I am trying to do here is to summarise a range of "typical" situations and use these to tie together the points made in earlier chapters.

Scenario 1: Browsing the Internet

In this scenario the client could be an individual sitting at home. They switch on their computer and contact their Internet Service Provider. This usually involves a dial-up or on cable systems the communication could be done using an IP address previously assigned by the cable company.

Once the ISP has been contacted and the initial information set up the client enters the URL to which they want to connect. This will be something like `http://www.boo.com`. Once this has been entered it is forwarded to the ISP's server. Name resolution now occurs and the server attempts to convert `www.boo.com` to an IP address. If this address is in its cache then the ISP server will reply from this. If the address is not in the cache the server will have to contact a DNS server and obtain the relevant IP address. Remember back to our DNS examples and appreciate that a number of DNS servers may have to be contacted before the final resolution is reached.

When the client machine receives the IP address it attempts to contact the Web server represented by the IP address. In this phase the ISP's server is initially contacted and the request is passed from router to router until the target machine is reached. Then, if all is well, the default HTML page is forwarded to the client and the usual process of "browsing" takes place.

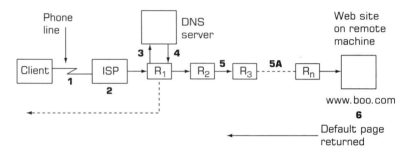

Steps

1 Client dials their ISP
2 Client enters URL of http://www.boo.com
3 ISP contacts local DNS server (additional lookups may be required or ISP server may have the data in cache)
4 DNS server returns IP address to the client
5 Client uses IP address from **4** to contact relevant server
    5A During this contact a number of routers have to be crossed. Each will move the data as in Chapter 2
6 The target Web server, once contacted, returns the default page to the client. From here the client moves using hyperlinks from page-to-page on the server

Figure 12.1 Browsing the Internet

In an attempt to simplify the client's user interface many browsers now accept the shortened URL format of www.xyz.com instead of having to prefix the domain name with http://. In this way it is hoped that the whole system will become simpler to use and understand. As more "simplifications" occur you can expect the precise sequence of events outlined above to change but the underlying principles remain the same.

Scenario 2: The Corporate Intranet

In this scenario the company has its own intranet and uses an internal Web server to convey information to the employees. This Web server is also supplied with information from the company's central database. The database could supply data concerning sales, products and other relevant factual content to the Web server.

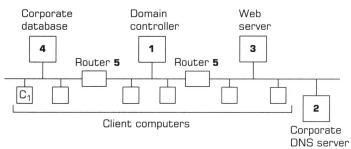

Steps

1 Client C_1 authenticates (logs on) to the domain controller
2 Client enters URL www.thiscompany.com to access the corporate Web server. This name is converted to an IP address by the corporate DNS server
3 The client uses the IP address to access the Web server
4 The company database automatically updates the Web server with new sales, product and client information
5 All data passes across the routers as in Chapter 2

Figure 12.2 The corporate intranet

A client logs onto the company network. This initial authentication is dealt with by the company domain controller. Once authenticated the client enters the URL of the corporate Web server into the browser. This could be something like www.thiscompany.com. Once this has been entered the name is passed to the company DNS server and is converted to the associated IP address. This address is used, as before, to enable the client to establish a connection with the Web server and obtain the relevant information in the usual way. Again, the data is passed across the routers using the same method as described in Chapter 2.

Should the network manager wish to, SNMP agents could be placed at any of the points 1, 2, 3, 4 or 5 in Figure 12.2. The manager could then, by sitting at one of the client computers, manage and control the network using the SNMP protocol. In this way network statistics could be prepared and presented from the raw data provided by the SNMP agents. These data could form the basis of network design decisions or other management considerations. In a well-integrated network the data could be automatically collated and published using the company Web server.

Scenario 3: The Corporate Intranet Connected to the Internet

This scenario is an extension of the previous one. Here there is an additional feature which is a connection to the outside world. We assume that the company maintains its own Internet Web server to provide outside users with information about its products.

In this example the area behind the proxy server (i.e., the network internal to the company) functions in exactly the same way as our previous setup. The major difference is in the way in which external clients view the company's site and how clients inside the company access the Internet.

In the case of an external client (as in Figure 12.3) trying to contact our Web server, their initial setup and access to the Internet is as in our first example. They type in the URL of our site (`www.thiscompany.com`) and this gives them access to our Web server. It is here that the firewall could act as a filtering device and only allow certain clients to access our Web server. In this way the system is acting like an extranet. If we allow all clients to access our site the network is acting as a "traditional" Web-based site. The role of the proxy server, at this point, is to stop all external clients from penetrating beyond the external Web server. In practice, additional security could be placed between the proxy server and the internal network to provide added safeguards.

Any documents or data that are going to be placed on the company's Web server can be done through the proxy server. By suitable configuration the proxy server and the Web server will allow certain groups or individuals to be able to add and modify data and HTML pages on the Web server. This will also apply to the corporate database. Modified data can therefore flow from the internal network to the Web server but not the other way round.

When an internal client contacts the Internet they type in the relevant URL. This is passed to the internal DNS server which compares its internal tables and its cache. If the URL can be matched to an IP address then that happens but otherwise the internal DNS server contacts an external

DNS server somewhere in the Internet. (This will usually be the ISP's main DNS server and is usually configured at setup). One of the external DNS servers will have the relevant IP address and this is passed back to both the client and the internal DNS server. In the latter case the entry is stored in the server's cache.

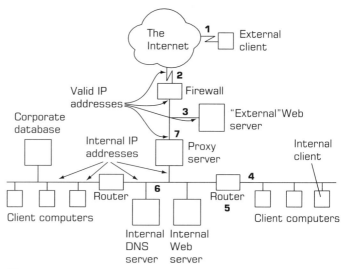

Figure 12.3
The Internet-
connected
corporate
intranet

Steps

1 External client connects to their ISP and enters a relevant URL (www.thiscompany.com)
2 The firewall allows/denies access (as required) to the Web server
3 Web server sends default page to client allowed through by the firewall
4 Internal client enters a URL
5 Internal router forwards this to the internal DNS server
6 Internal DNS server resolves name to get an IP address (it may have to contact an external DNS server to do this)
7 Once an IP address is obtained, the request to open the URL is passed to the proxy server. This takes the internal (source) IP address and substitutes this for the proxy server's valid IP address

The client takes this IP address and contacts the proxy server which forwards the data to the Internet after it has substituted its valid IP address for the client's internal address. In this way the proxy server masquerades as the client as far as the Internet is concerned. The proxy server continues this IP address conversion as data moves between the internal and external networks. Apart from this, the data transfer works in exactly the same way as in our previous examples.

Scenario 4: Individual e-mail

Figure 12.4 shows the situation with regards to simple e-mail. By this I mean the typical e-mail setup by which most of us communicate across the Internet.

Figure 12.4
Simple e-mail

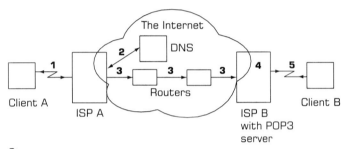

Steps

1 Client A creates some e-mail. This is forwarded (sent) to their ISP

2 The ISP checks the FQDN of the recipient e.g., fred@xyz.com. If the matching IP address is known it is used. If it is not known then one or more DNS servers are contacted to resolve the address

3 Once the IP address is known, the e-mail is forwarded across the Internet in the usual fashion

4 The recipient's ISP stores the e-mail in their POP server

5 Client B "dials-up" their ISP. The POP server informs them that they have mail

In this scenario the first client, Client A, composes some mail. They then press the "send" button or initiate the send mail routine in their browser. The e-mail is then transferred to their ISP. The receiving SMTP system checks the location of the recipient by looking at the FQDN component of the e-mail. If the recipient is something like bill@sales.big-company.com the system will look up sales.bigcompany.com in the usual way. If the associated IP address is held by the local DNS server this address is used. If the address cannot be found the system contacts an external DNS server and resolves the name as before.

Once the associated IP address is known the e-mail data (the message) is transferred across the Internet by a series of "hops" until the recipient's ISP is reached. Here the incoming e-mail is stored on a POP (Post Office Protocol) server. This acts as a message store until the receiving client, Client B, dials-in and the POP server informs them that they have mail. The system will then download the mail and they can then deal with it in the usual way. Some more modern systems use a modified protocol and this allows them to decide prior to download which parts of their e-mail they wish to keep.

The same principles work in corporate e-mail with the difference that each department will usually manage their own mail server. Remember that most mail systems use an SMTP (Simple Mail Transfer Protocol) server to forward mail and a POP (Post Office Protocol) server to store mail. These are usually located on the same machine. Figure 12.5 illustrates the principles of corporate e-mail.

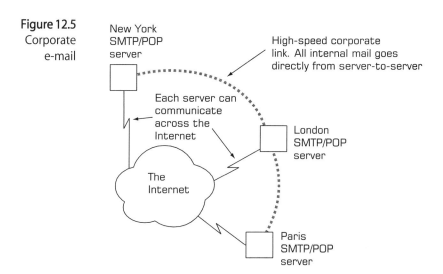

Figure 12.5
Corporate
e-mail

New York SMTP/POP server

High-speed corporate link. All internal mail goes directly from server-to-server

Each server can communicate across the Internet

London SMTP/POP server

The Internet

Paris SMTP/POP server

Scenario 5: Electronic Banking

Electronic banking is rapidly becoming one of the growth areas of Internet traffic. By using this an account holder is able to check balances, move money and pay bills from anywhere in the world.

Each bank has its own proprietary implementation of security systems. The illustration outlined here is a composite of a number of different methods used around the world. The essential principle is to guarantee secrecy and to ensure that if data is intercepted at any one part of the process it will be in a form that will not allow the "eavesdropper" to gain access to the account.

In some situations the password, PIN, and account number can be augmented with a physical device such as a magnetic "swipe card". This is attached to the client's machine and will allow a higher degree of access to the account than the password/PIN combination alone.

Figure 12.6 Illustrates the *principles* in such a transaction

Here the client initiates the whole process by contacting the bank's server. Prior to this the client has had an account set up and will have received, usually by post, the PIN number and password to give access to the account. In most cases the initial PIN number and password have been generated by the bank. The client must change them the first time they connect to the bank's server. The server stores these items in an encrypted format and these encrypted details are only accessible by trusted staff members in the bank.

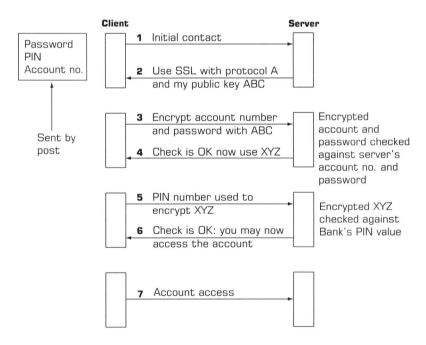

Figure 12.6   Secure transactions

When the client contacts the bank's server the server instructs the client to use the secure sockets layer (SSL) communication. This phase is invisible to the client and during this machine-to-machine negotiation the specific protocol that will be used to encrypt the data is decided upon.

In many secure software implementations there is usually an additional phase in the protection of important data. An illustration of the type of process follows: Imagine that the initial protocols have been decided. The server then sends a random number (xyz in our example) to the client computer. The client is then asked for their account number and the associated password. Rather than have the system pass both of these "across" the Internet the client uses the account number and password to encrypt the random number and this encrypted data is sent back to the server. Since the server has copies of all the client's information it can apply the same algorithm to its copy of the random number and if the result matches what the client has sent then the client is assumed to have passed the initial check.

A similar, but different, method is then used to obtain the client's PIN number. If both of these processes check out the client is allowed access to their account. The important points are as follows:

1. The account number, initial PIN, and initial password are generated quite separately to the "electronic" process used to connect to the server.

2. By using a random integer and passing an encrypted form of this across the network at no time is any of the vital account information sent in "clear text" across the Internet.

3. By forcing two separate validations each separated by a few seconds any "eavesdropper" has to capture both sessions to even begin to obtain information about the accounts and the codes necessary to access them.

As stated earlier, all of the above could be further implemented by additional security measures, should these be deemed necessary.

Throughout this chapter I have tried to outline the major areas in which the different parts of the Internet are currently used. The future holds a great deal more for these systems. The evolution of streaming video, streaming audio and high-bandwidth mobile telephones are just a few of the areas where this technology is set to expand rapidly.

Even allowing for this expansion most of the technologies outlined in this chapter will continue to work in much the same way over the next few years. Watch this space!

Chapter 13

Establishing your Domain Name and Web Presence

Why do I Need to Register?

We have seen throughout the previous chapters that the Internet is really a collection of different computer systems, all of which speak the "language" of TCP/IP. As the popularity of the Internet grows and more companies advertise using the virtual shopfront, it becomes increasingly likely that the average family, or small business, will want to establish some kind of "Web presence".

In the next few paragraphs we will see how this can be done. In my examples I will use the BTConnect service (now renamed BTClick). This has been my first choice for a number of reasons but please remember that almost all Internet Service Providers allow this sort of facility. It is simply a case of determining which of these companies provides the best overall package for you or your business. When looking at what each ISP offers make sure that you check out any hidden costs such as:

- A "free" service that charges £45 per hour for telephone support;
- A "free" service that is so busy during "normal" working hours that it is unusable.

Also, try to get a feel for how straightforward their registration process is. All too often what looks like a simple, easy-to-use system is bedevilled by inconsistencies coupled with support staff who themselves do not know what to do.

What is entailed in this process? Quite simply the ISP (Internet Service Provider) agrees, for a fee, to reserve space on their DNS server for your FQDN (Fully Qualified Domain Name). In doing this they will also provide services to host (allow you to use) space on their Web server and also to allow you to use your own e-mail address. They will also register you as the holder of this FQDN and prevent anyone else from using the name.

Let us illustrate this by using the fictitious FQDN of myhouse2.org.uk

Figure 13.1 shows the fact that prior to registration the higher-level servers (in a DNS sense) are unable to locate the new domain.

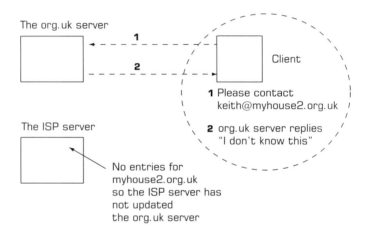

Figure 13.1　Before registering myhouse2.org.uk

Figure 13.2 shows that after the registration process the higher-level servers can resolve (find) the IP address of the domain myhouse2.org.uk; how does this registration come about? Let us look at this from the perspective of a user who wishes to register their family name or company name as a new Internet domain.

Initially, an Internet user will contact their ISP. The ISP will usually have an introduction screen that allows a user to find out if a domain name is available. In our example our user would type myhouse2.org.uk and ask the system to check the availability of this name. Not surprisingly, in our example, the system will tell them that the domain name is available. The length of time taken for the search will vary depending on the type of name requested. Generally speaking, searching, from within

Europe, for any name ending with .com, .net or .org will take longer than the corresponding search for .org.uk or .co.uk names and so on. The reason for this is that USA-style names have to be checked with the UK *and* US registration agencies; a process which takes time.

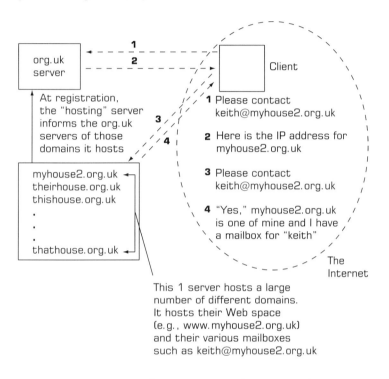

Figure 13.2   After registering myhouse2.org.uk

Once we have decided to register myhouse2.org.uk, and agree to pay the relevant fee, we will be asked a series of questions about our e-mail addresses and our Web site. For their part the ISP will have to inform a number of the higher-level servers about the fact that the new domain is being hosted (managed) by them. This process also takes time and it is about 24 to 36 hours before our name and the associated e-mail addresses can be used. This 24- to 36-hour period is the time it takes for the details of our domain to be copied across all of the relevant servers. Once the higher-level domain servers know about this they will propagate this information amongst themselves so that any other Internet user will be able to find us. Figures 13.3 to 13.9 show this registration process for BTConnect.

Figure 13.3

The entry screen to allow us to search for our domain name

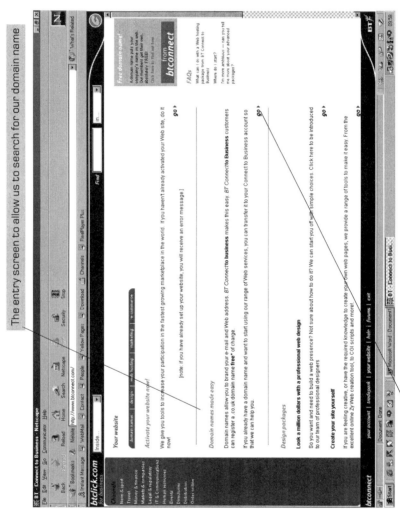

Having decided on a domain we use this option to go to the next screen

Figure 13.4

Following on from the previous screen (Figure 13.3) we enter the prefix
of the domain we would like to register

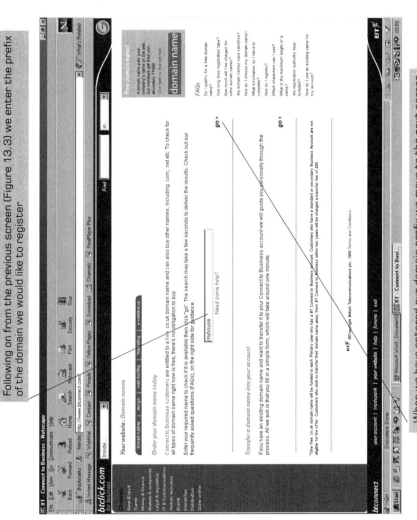

When we have entered our domain prefix we move to the next screen

Figure 13.5

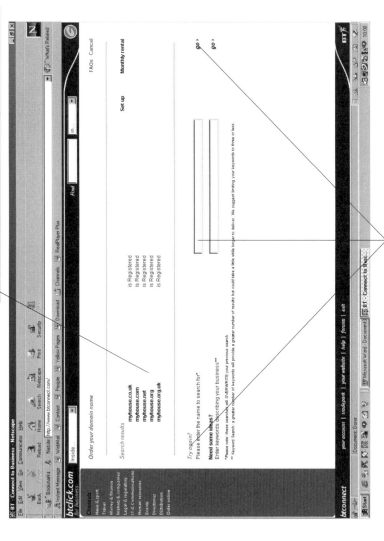

Figure 13.6

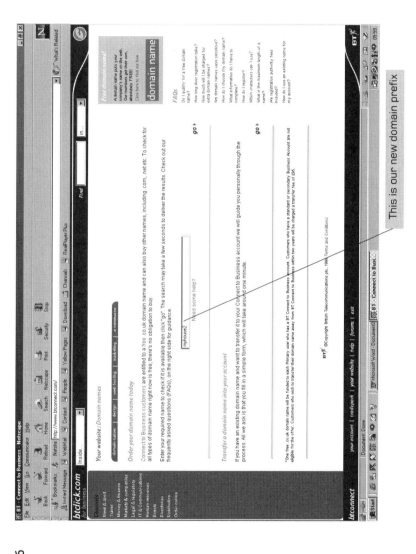

Figure 13.7

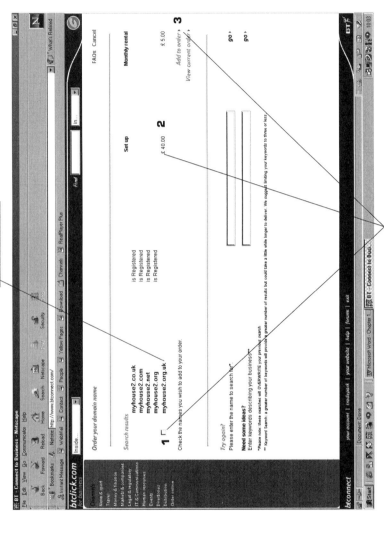

One is available

Select Box **1**, incur fee **2** and proceed with **3**

Figure 13.8

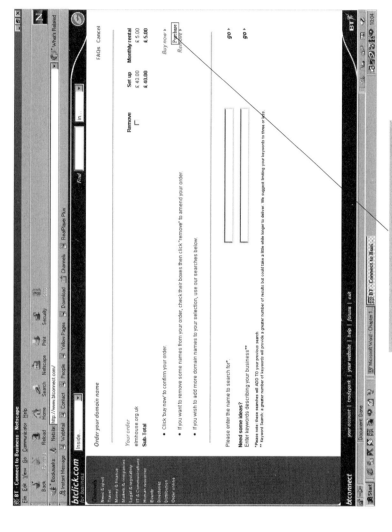

To confirm the purchase select "Buy now"

Figure 13.9

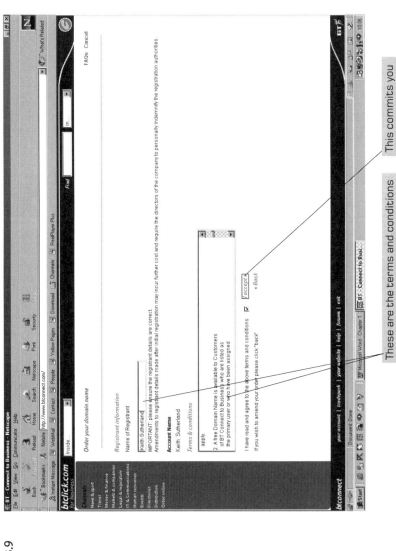

Initially, we try to register the domain name myhouse only to find that the range of valid suffixes (.co.uk, .org.uk, etc.) are all registered. We return to the search screen and enter the name myhouse2. Many of the domain names are also registered but myhouse2.org.uk is still available. This will suit our purposes so we proceed.

At the end of this process we will have to wait the 24 to 36 hours for the DNS entries to be updated and the space set aside on the ISP's Web server. During this time our ISP will inform the relevant "higher-level" DNS servers that the FQDN myhouse2.org.uk exists and is registered on their machine.

Once all of this has taken place, all that is left for us to do is to design our Web site using any of the currently available packages and then upload the site to our ISP host. The details of how to do this vary from one ISP to another and these details change quite often. Please check with your ISP to find out the exact steps that need to be taken. BTConnect have a number or reasonably automated procedures for creating a general Web site. If you want something more sophisticated you will either have to create one yourself or pay for a professional design bureau to create one for you.

Once we have established our Web site it is necessary for us to inform as many search engines as possible about our Web site. This is less important if the site is a family one but it is vital if we want our business "on the Web". Some ISPs will do this for you – for a fee. The alternative is to download some of the automatic programs that will do this; a number can be found at:

www.bhs.com   (**Note:** this is *not* the department store!)

A number of others are available from the utilities Web sites whose URLs are listed at the end of this book. Additionally, your ISP may have a number of options for doing this – be careful though, some ISPs charge substantial fees for this service.

What Exactly *is* a Search Engine?

Quite simply, it is a database of Web sites that is maintained by an organisation to assist in finding information "on the Web". Many of these databases have their own search facilities – hence the name. Examples are Yahoo, Lycos, Excite and AltaVista. The URLs for some of the more common search engines are listed at the end of this book.

Typically, these search engines started life as experimental sites of either private groups or corporations and they now pay for themselves through advertising revenues or simply by enhancing the reputation of the companies that manage them. Each of the search engines have a bias towards a particular type of information. Yahoo, Excite and Lycos tend to be for "modern and trendy" information: music, fashion and so on, whereas AltaVista is very good for text-based or factual searches. In general, you need to use a search engine that is suited to, and geared towards, the type of information that you require. If you cannot find information on one particular search engine it pays to try the search on another one, preferably one that searches using a different method. If Yahoo fails then try Excite or AltaVista. Quite often, one of the search engines will find information that a number of others have failed to locate. In the same way, getting your Web site onto a relevant search engine can greatly assist anyone trying to find your company on the Web.

After doing this we have our own domain name and our own Web site but what about e-mail? At the time of writing, the current offer from BTConnect is 20 e-mail addresses for each domain name. This number can be increased for corporate registrations but, of course, you pay more! The 20 e-mail address deal is ideal for the smaller business or family so we could register the following family members:

```
fred@myhouse2.org.uk
sue@myhouse2.org.uk
jim@myhouse2.org.uk
```

And so on. Clearly, the choice of e-mail address and domain name needs to be thought out clearly before committing to this process. A sensible name can enhance your "Web presence" but a clumsy or ill-conceived name can remain with you for a long time. The BTConnect menus are generally well thought out and the support staff are quite helpful. They make the whole process as easy as possible.

Once all this has been done, all that is needed is a regular update of your Web site to keep it fresh and relevant!

Chapter 14

The Future of IP

Staring into crystal balls in an attempt to discern future trends is a dangerous occupation. That said, I will try to show some of the future developments that are under way within the Internet community and to impart to the reader what these changes are likely to mean to the typical user. The information is presented in the form of a news bulletin rather than an in-depth investigation.

IP V6

Back in the early 1990s the guiding bodies of the Internet community felt that the number of available IP addresses was running out. This was due to the rapid growth in popularity of the Internet and also down to the fact that some of the methods used to allocate IP address ranges to organisations were very inefficient. Due to the methods in use at the time, a company requiring a few hundred addresses for their computers would get a network address for some 65,000 machines. Those addresses the company did not require would simply be "wasted".

The sheer growth in demand for IP addresses and the additional demands made by the strong graphical content of many Web sites have both contributed to the problems. These factors, together with the growth of audio and video used by these sites, made the Internet designers look for ways of meeting the, then current, requirements and also the likely future needs of the Internet community. They concluded that the very address structure of the Internet needed to be changed.

In short, the new Internet Protocol, IP version 6, uses a 128-bit address structure as opposed to the current 32-bit structure (four times longer) and this gives enough IP addresses for almost every square centimetre of planet surface! It is hoped that this will meet all current and future demands!

In addition to providing more addresses Ipv6, as it is called, also has provision for controlling things like video and audio quality and better in-built security mechanisms. This means that it is ideally suited to services like Internet telephones and Internet cinema.

There are many issues associated with the implementation of Ipv6. Its very address structure makes it complex to introduce and now the implementers have an added difficulty in that the current version of IP, version 4, is seen by many people to be quite acceptable. The problem is that the newer system and the older system will have to co-exist for some time before we say farewell to the "much loved" Ipv4.

Ipv6 will, however, change many aspects of the way in which we use the Internet making it possible for each of us to have a personal and mobile IP address. Not only that but our home heating system, lighting, television etc., could also have an associated IP address and therefore be controllable from wherever we are.

If the current version is Ipv4 and the newer version is Ipv6 whatever happened to IP version 5? The answer is that this was simply a test system used in laboratories around the world. It was never intended for general release. Ipv6 will make its presence felt during the next few years. Eventually we are all likely to use some aspects of Ipv6 in our communications.

Multicast IP

One of the ideas behind Ipv4 was that a single source should be able to send data out to a number of recipients at the same time. Many of the Ipv4 systems use an address broadcasting system. This means that one piece of equipment transmits some data and that this data is received by all other pieces of equipment on the local network. While this works for data transfer it is not suited to corporate teleconferencing or for home cinema. How would one charge for a cinema service if all customers could access the films by default? Similarly, how could a company feel confident in the integrity of its conferencing if all computers on the Internet could "listen in".

The answer lies in multicasting. By this method one computer transmits data and only those in the "multicast group" would be able to receive the data. Group membership could be controlled by some security mechanism (public key perhaps) and to join a group you would have to pay or be a member of the approved group (the board of a company or the members of a club). Only with a valid group membership will you be able to access the media made available to that multicast group.

Trials of multicast media have existed for some time. The current limitation is the bandwidth issue, or how much data can be forced down our phone lines. Until some new technologies evolve we will be unable to exploit the full potential of multicast data systems.

Voice and Video Over IP

Voice and video over IP also tend to suffer from the same problems as multicasting of data. In theory it should be possible over many systems to send real-time talk and/or video. The reality is that the existing Internet was developed to transfer data across the world. Because of this the system can, as it transmits the data, split the data up into many different parts and send each part separately. At the data-receiving end the computer reassembles these parts into our document or message. While this works fine for text-based messages it does not work too well for pictures or sound. These need to be received in sequence and at a speed that seems "life-like".

Ipv6 addresses some of these "quality" issues. Once again, one of the major factors is the amount of available bandwidth. Until this is resolved then many of the proposed extensions to the IP system remain in the realms of the IP research laboratories. With the large number of people working on the different solutions to this problem it will not be long before we are able to talk to and see the person at the other end of the internet "phone". The quality will be determined by the amount of available bandwidth that the link has.

Mobile IP

Anyone who has used their portable computer and their mobile phone to send and receive e-mail will know that it is painfully slow. The problem is that the original wireless phone standards never envisaged the use of such devices to transmit data. While our home and office computer systems send and receive data at a rate of 56,600 bps (or greater) the poor old mobile phone is limited to 9,600 bps. This seemed more than adequate some 20 years ago but is now hopelessly inadequate.

What is needed is a new wireless data communication standard. This is coming and the recent flurry of press speculation about the allocation of "mobile IP" licenses shows how close this new standard is to being implemented.

Secondary to the question of the speed of data transfer is the technical requirement of mobile IP. Let us discuss what this means.

Imagine that Ipv6 has been implemented and that each one of us has their own IP address. This is a personal IP address and enables us, should we have the correct technology, to send and receive e-mail from wherever we are in the world. Suppose we are based in London and have an arrangement with a London ISP. All is fine while we are in the "catchment" area of London. When we travel abroad with our own, personal, IP address we will be sending and receiving messages and data through our mobile phone or our mobile phone connected to our portable computer. Either way it is the same problem.

Let us say that we travel to Los Angeles. Our mobile communication device now has to contact a Los Angeles supplier and say to them: "Hello, this is my IP address. Please would you route all e-mail for me from London to my temporary location in Los Angeles". In the same way that our mobile phones establish connections throughout Europe and route our calls backwards and forwards so too will we be able to reroute data through these new systems.

There are a number of problems to be overcome. These involve security: when the London ISP receives a request from the Los Angeles ISP to reroute all e-mail for a user to the new location, how does London know it is genuine and not a hoax? Should I be able to carry out telephone conversations and accept video data, how are the billing costs arranged? These problems and a number of other technological "knots" are currently being worked on. Fairly soon we will have one, or a number of, personal communication devices and these will follow us, and our personal IP address, around the globe.

While waiting for Ipv6 to emerge, a number of enterprising companies have taken to providing a range of services that are available through our mobile phones. This range of services is called WAP (Wireless Application Protocol). They are intended to deliver, to our mobile phones and other communications equipment, a simplified range of services currently found on "normal" Web-access devices. At the time of writing the functionality of these services is quite limited. Delivering data to mobile phones requires a high degree of bandwidth and good service provision. These early attempts to get such data delivered should be seen as the first early steps towards a fully mobile Internet. We will not see useful functionality until the new generation of mobile phones arrive and quite possibly not until the uptake of Ipv6 on this new system.

ADSL and Other Technologies

Traditionally, the established telecoms companies have had a major problem. By being amongst the first to lay down the complex networks of copper cables they are now suffering because the established system has to be kept going at the same time as the introduction of all the new technologies that people are demanding. In many ways the two systems are mutually exclusive.

ISDN, which many people feel is a "new technology", has actually been around for almost 25 years. The only thing that stopped it from being accepted is that, until the arrival of the Internet, there was no need for it. It was, literally, a solution in search of a problem! Now it is the recommended method of moving data for a home or office Internetwork.

ISDN offers 64 kilobits (thousand bits) of data transfer. If you are lucky and there is low congestion on the telephone system, and you have the right communications equipment, you may get 128 kilobits per second (Kbps). If you manage to achieve 128 Kbps it is unlikely that this rate of data transfer will last for long. The problem is that the older "telephone-based" communications system cannot cope with the demand for data transfer rates made by all the users.

One of the newer technologies due for "imminent release" is ADSL (Asynchronous Digital Subscriber Lines). This technology, which runs over modern telephone lines, delivers between 512 kilobits and 2 megabits of data transfer per second. It can handle more than this but this is the probable maximum when the system is released some time in spring/summer 2000. There will be different rates of upload and download but overall the user will see a very considerable rate of increase in the general responsiveness of the data transfer mechanism. Other, faster, technological developments are "just around the corner". Once this technology is established users will have far more capacity for video and audio connection to the Internet.

The only thing that is guaranteed is that the future Internet will be more flexible, more varied and a greater part of our day-to-day lives than anyone can imagine.

Napster

Recently, an innovation in Internet technologies has caught the public's attention. Napster is one of the first, publicly available, programs to employ distributed technology and, as a result of this, the first to seriously threaten some major industries in a way which appears to bypass the normal legal protections that they historically enjoy.

What exactly does Napster offer? Let us look at the "traditional" way in which, say, music files would be made available to the Internet user. Figure 14.1 illustrates this. Here we have a central server acting as a "library" of stored music files. This arrangement can be used in a number of ways. A typical scenario is as follows: A user logs onto the centralised Web site and fills in some forms which give membership to the site. The user can now download the files they want from the site. The site itself will have links to other, similar, sites and this interconnection of sites allows additional resources to be accessed.

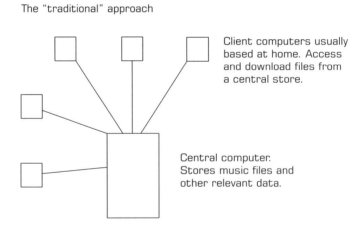

The "traditional" approach

Client computers usually based at home. Access and download files from a central store.

Central computer. Stores music files and other relevant data.

Figure 14.1 The "traditional" approach

From the legal point of view the above scenario can be easily stopped. Most countries have copyright laws and any site offering unlawfully copied data can find itself subject to very strong legal action – likely to result in closure of the site and prosecution of the site's owners.

Figure 14.2 illustrates the Napster version of the above site. The central site now no longer holds the data files but simply provides a means whereby other Napster users can access each other's data. In this way the central site is acting as a "gatekeeper" and allows members of the same "club" to access files held by other members of the "club". It is the computer equivalent of a private club whereby members have access to each other's collections of, typically, music files. They can share these files and both copy and distribute them freely around member's computers.

The Napster approach

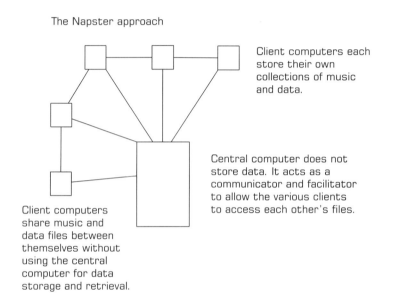

Client computers each store their own collections of music and data.

Central computer does not store data. It acts as a communicator and facilitator to allow the various clients to access each other's files.

Client computers share music and data files between themselves without using the central computer for data storage and retrieval.

Figure 14.2   The Napster approach

The legal problem is that there is no centralised "store" of illegally copied data. The music industry – primarily because it is currently the industry most affected by this development – is now faced with the task of pursuing a number of individuals rather than one central organisation.

Napster currently offers two major innovations. Firstly, a threat to the record industry. This will be dealt with by revised legislation and possibly a modification in the way that the music industry does business. Secondly, a completely new way in which people think of their computers and their connections across the Internet. It will not be long before "Napster-like" programs allow groups of users with similar interests to create dynamic, evolving, groups through which to share information and data files as easily as exchanging photos in a family "get together". We will see the emergence of Internet Communities sharing common interests and exchanging sound, video and data files as freely as we now exchange e-mail.

More information on Napster can be obtained from:

```
www.napster.com
```

Chapter 15

WAP, UMTS and Bluetooth

The Future

During the time of writing this book there has been a great deal of talk about the new "wireless" Internet. At the moment this technology is in its infancy but it promises to deliver a great deal to a potentially new and very large audience. Three important new technologies underpin this "wireless" revolution:

- **WAP** (Wireless Application Protocol) – provides the equivalent of the traditional HTML-based Web applications and services;
- **UMTS** (Universal Mobile Telecommunications System) – the new 3G (third generation) mobile phone standard providing greater bandwidth and increased functionality to the mobile phone; and
- **Bluetooth** – both an industry consortium and a new technology aimed at providing wireless local networks for the home and business.

The three together seem likely to make up the core systems of tomorrow's wireless Internet.

The current population of computer users is quite large (approximately one in three households in the UK, slightly more in the USA and in Germany). The population of mobile phone users is much higher and the phone population is growing even faster than the computer population. A marketing department's dream is therefore to combine the different populations of users and make the Internet accessible to all users. Unfortunately, there are one or two technical problems with this simplistic approach.

In general, computer users want full-screen graphics; they are prepared to put up with the dialling time that their computers take to connect to the Internet and they are reasonably tolerant of situations where the "egg-timer" tells them they have to wait for an unspecified period of time for some process to happen. This is all endured in return for full-screen colour graphics and some sound and video delivery.

The phone users tend to be an impatient lot. They want connectivity when they switch their phones on and they want access to information relatively quickly and without having to type in URLs (Web addresses such as www.xyz.com). These requirements, combined with the limitation of a very small screen (even the enlarged display on some phones is seriously limited compared to a 17- or 19-inch computer monitor) mean that the designers of the various WAP systems have had to rethink some aspects of the technology.

At the "nuts and bolts" end of the technology TCP/IP is a rather inefficient method of delivering information across a wireless medium. TCP/IP was, as we have seen, based around early long-distance telephone connections and as such does not lend itself to wireless delivery. With TCP/IP most information is transferred as text with lots of checks and balances to ensure reliable delivery. This "overhead" adds up to a somewhat cumbersome delivery system which takes up too much of the available bandwidth on mobile phones.

So, for wireless Internet connectivity to work satisfactorily, a new approach is called for. This new approach has to cover the user interface and also has to improve the mechanisms by which the data is delivered to the user's handset. What is required is a rethink of the way in which our old friend HTML allows us to present information to the Web browser.

New Markup Languages

To recap: HTML is a text markup language. It allows us to mark pieces of text as "Heading", "Title", "Table" and so on and also to embed graphics into our page. When the Web server is contacted by the client this text-based page is downloaded to the client's browser. Typically, the user reads the page and clicks on the next reference. This is possibly a "hyperlink" (a link to another page on a different computer system). The client computer then contacts the relevant server and downloads another page of text-based material. As the user continues to "surf" the Internet each successive page is downloaded with each download proceeded by the client computer contacting the Web server and requesting the relevant page.

This constant contacting of the server by the client and all of the associated communications overhead results in a less-than-efficient means of data delivery. In the past this lack of efficiency was offset by the reliability of such a system. Remember: originally, almost all traffic carried by the Internet was carried by long-distance telephone connections. These tended to be noisy and somewhat unreliable. The system has improved considerably over recent years.

With WAP-based screens the structure of the information is considerably more ordered. This allows the user to step through a series of pre-defined choices with a carefully constructed display of information at each stage. Therefore, there is no need for a mouse-based pointer system; the WAP user can navigate through the screens using the arrow keys on the handset.

To enable these simpler, more structured, screens the WAP system does away with the traditional "Web page" approach and uses a series of simpler pages called *cards*. A group of cards is organised into a *deck* and this deck is what is downloaded onto the mobile phone. As a user moves from one card to another the phone does not have to contact the server for each change. Only when moving outside the cards within the deck does the phone have to contact the server for another deck.

With a carefully constructed WAP site, sensibly structured decks and an intuitive layout of cards, the number of times that a user will have to contact the server can be reduced considerably. This also has the effect of reducing the "overhead" associated with a traditional "Web site".

Figures 15.1 and 15.2 show the principle behind this process. By reducing both the quantity of data and the quantity of control information flowing from the WAP gateway, the efficiency of the whole data transfer process is improved. By increasing this overall efficiency the WAP community hope to provide more effective data-transmission rates than their land-line equivalents can deliver. Current estimates state that WAP-enabled devices require approximately one-eighth of the data overhead of their more traditional counterparts.

Should the WAP developers succeed in achieving these efficiencies and proving that they have a better way of delivering data to the end-user's equipment it will only be a matter of time before these technologies will be adopted by the "traditional" Internet community. Should this happen we will see our common HTML-based Web server being replaced by its WAP counterpart.

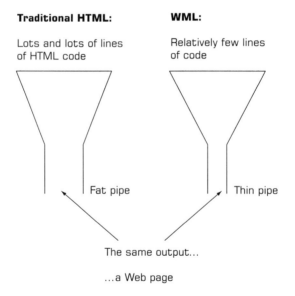

WAP-enabled Web server

<head
Hello </head>
<p>
A message

HTML text output
from a Web server.

**WAP-enabled
mobile phone**

1.

10010010

2.

Standard HTML on the
Web server is translated
into binary by the WAP gateway.
This reduces the size of the data
and improves transmission times.

Converted
into binary by the
gateway and sent
to the mobile
phone.

WAP gateway

Figure 15.1

Traditional HTML:

Lots and lots of lines
of HTML code

WML:

Relatively few lines
of code

Fat pipe

Thin pipe

The same output...

...a Web page

Figure 15.2

While all of the above developments mean that the delivery system to the WAP devices will be more efficient and provide a better use of the available bandwidth, it does not address the problems of the user interface and of the somewhat confused Web sites that fill the Internet. To deal with these problems and to enhance the benefits offered by the improved delivery system WAP site designers must structure the way in which the Web sites deliver information. To do this they have redesigned the way in which the typical page of information is sent to the receiving device. As stated earlier: In the original method of delivery this information is sent a page at a time with each graphic being sent as a separate "package".

As we have seen, with the WAP approach a Web site is organised as a series of decks and cards. Each deck contains a number of cards. When a user contacts a WAP site it is no longer the default *page* that gets downloaded it is the default *deck*. As the user moves from one card to another it is no longer necessary to download each page from the server. All of the immediate data requirements are met by the data within the deck. This process is illustrated in Figure 15.3.

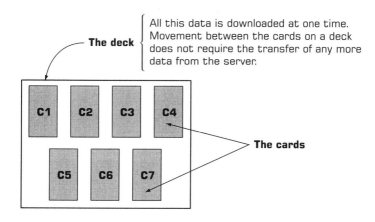

Figure 15.3

By carefully structuring the deck it is only necessary to transfer new data when a new deck is required – not as each new page, or card, is accessed. Fundamental to this process is the design of efficient WAP sites and essential to this design is the presence of a markup language structured for such a purpose.

The WAP developers are currently producing a highly evolved version of the HTML markup language. Currently, most WAP development is done using either XML (eXtended Markup Language) or by using early versions of WML (Wap Markup Language). These should be seen as highly evolved versions of the "traditional" markup language which allow the development of these more efficient and more structured Web sites.

By a combination of carefully constructed decks and cards and by using binary-data transfer – rather than the current text-based data formats – the WAP developers promise to revolutionise the way in which we access our data. By the same token they intend to make this data more easily accessible to a much wider population than before. Should they even partially succeed then these efficiencies will find their way into the way in which "traditional" Internet systems transfer information and we will be soon be using these WAP technologies as part of our standard Internet systems.

New Mobile Telephone Systems

UMTS stands for Universal Mobile Telecommunications System. It is a central part of the International Telecommunications Union's plan for a "third generation" (3G) communication system that will integrate voice, data and video. This will provide us with handsets (mobile phones) that are capable of sending and receiving whatever range of data services we want to and from anywhere in the world. UMTS is the central plank in a series of technologies that will enable world-wide multimedia communications for the estimated 2 *billion*+ users, across the whole planet, by 2010.

As it currently stands UMTS will provide data rates up to 2Mbps (as opposed to the current 9600bps) with global roaming (you can use the phone anywhere) and a wide range of integrated data and multimedia services. In Europe the current round of "third generation" phone licences are being issued. The huge prices paid for these licences in the UK show what most of the companies involved think are the likely rewards of these technologies. Currently, UMTS has the support of several hundred manufacturers, network operators other service providers.

Wireless Networks in the Home and Office

One of the major problems affecting the small office or home network user is the fact that the cabling and equipment provision and maintenance required for such an activity can be quite a daunting task for the typical user.

How much simpler then if all the components of one's equipment contacted each other when it was switched on and simply transmitted data over a wireless medium, similar to a short-wave "walkie-talkie" system.

Bluetooth is another industry consortium that aims to do just that. In a

"Bluetooth" household computer equipment and many home appliances will register themselves with each other and transfer data to and from themselves without the requirement of wires, hubs, switches etc.

This range of technologies means that in a Bluetooth interactive conference, documents, business cards and presentations will be transferred between computers without any wired connections.

By using the same technology it would be possible for your mobile phone to function in three different ways. At home it will function as a normal wireless phone and you will pay a standard line charge as you would for using your ordinary household phone. When you are on the move it will work as an ordinary mobile phone. When at home and/or within range of other phones with Bluetooth technology built in it will function as a walkie-talkie and incur no line charges.

Bluetooth has the full backing of a large number of major industry players. Within the next few years a large number of Bluetooth devices will make themselves available and start to change the way in which the traditional network is implemented; and by its ease of use enable many more businesses and households to enjoy network connectivity.

More information on all of the technologies outlined above can be found on the following Web sites:

```
http://www.umts-forum.org
http://www.wapforum.org
http://www.bluetooth.com
```

Appendix A

The Physical Structure of the Internet

Increasingly, I have been asked questions along the lines of "But how does my data get from London to, say, Toronto?" To fully grasp how this happens it is necessary to have an understanding not just of the technologies involved but also something of the physical structure of the Internet. For reasons of simplification, in some of the following paragraphs I have combined examples from both the United States of America and the models usually found in European cities.

To comprehend this physical structure let us examine the recent rapid growth of the Internet from the perspective of the various service suppliers and telecommunications companies that are involved.

Back in the mid-1980s the Internet was becoming congested. A major rearrangement of high-volume traffic carriers was needed. The NSF (National Science Foundation) of the USA started investigating alternative forms of suitable designs. It created NSFNET and this connected various 56 Kbps lines in the United States. This speed (56 thousand bits per second) was then considered to be very fast. During the following five years the basic design proved successful and the speed of the connections was steadily increased. At about this time the various telecommunications companies started to see the potential of the Internet and offered to support the growth of the infrastructure in return for a proportion of any revenues, hopefully, so produced. This was timely since the NSF realised that the size of the project had grown beyond its funding means.

In 1990 the NSF started the process of making the Internet a commercial enterprise and they, together with the various telecommunications companies, upgraded the NSFNET network to run at 45 Mbps. This speed (45 million bits per second) is now considered quite moderate for a major service!

By 1992 plans were in place to supersede the NSFNET design with one that provided more potential for growth and flexibility for the future demands of the Internet community.

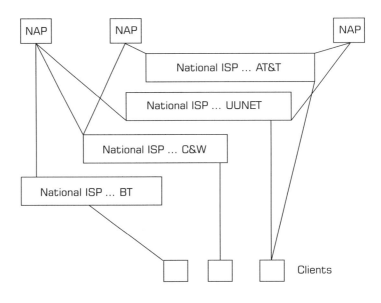

Figure A1

Figure A1 shows, in outline, the initial design. Any company that has the ability to carry a major proportion of Internet traffic is said to be a *backbone provider*. By "backbone" we mean a major network infrastructure which can carry a high-volume of traffic and allow other smaller networks to connect to it. Typically, the backbone providers have all been the traditional telecommunications companies. The backbone providers (AT&T, MCI, IBM, etc.) connected their networks at structures called NAPs (Network Access Points). These worked like high-speed exchanges, in a traditional telecommunications sense.

Companies connecting into these NAPs agreed to do two things. Firstly, to exchange traffic with some backbone providers (we will now call them National Internet Service Providers) and secondly to sell transit services to other national ISPs. In this way AT&T might well exchange traffic with BT but sell part of their network capability to smaller organisations who could easily sell on some surplus capacity to their clients. The exchange of traffic information is called *peering* and was usually done by organisations of roughly the same size and without money changing hands. This "reciprocal" arrangement meant that the organisations involved gained the benefits of the increased infrastructure and could pass on to their clients the benefits of the increased network capability. The clients would, of course, pay for this extra service. The initial NAPs were all paid for by the NSF.

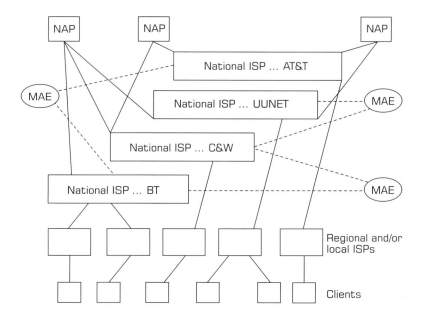

Figure A2

As demand grew groups of the larger telecommunications companies started putting in their own dedicated NAPs. These were called Metropolitan Access Exchanges (MAEs). With this capability BT and Cable & Wireless could provide a couple of MAEs to improve the flow of traffic across their networks. In structure and function an MAE is the same as a NAP but funded by commercial organisations. Figure A2 illustrates this stage.

At this point in development the system is now able to offer smaller organisations the ability to provide local services and direct the traffic from these into the major backbones provided by the large telecommunications companies. Individual clients can choose to connect to a smaller (local town) ISP or directly into a service provided by one of the major players.

Traditionally, a local ISP would have to provide some degree of infrastructure. They would have to put in cables, routers, high-speed switches and other equipment. This would enable them to offer services to subscribers and thereby give them the connection into the major networks.

In an attempt to simplify this process many major providers now offer a process called Virtual ISP (vISP). To illustrate this let us imagine a medium-sized grocery chain. They wish to provide online ordering and associated services but do not want to make the investment in staff, equipment and infrastructure that would be required if they were to become a traditional ISP. One of the major service providers offer to do this for them. The grocery chain now offers its customers "free" Internet access, it pays the major ISP for this service, and uses this, Internet access provision, to attract advertisers and as a vehicle to promote its major business.

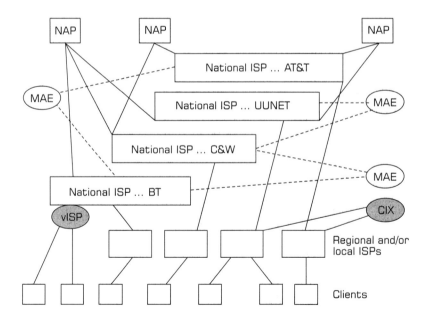

Figure A3

The client appears to be connecting into a separate physical infrastructure but is actually connecting to a part of an established major ISP. The major ISP gains by charging the grocery chain for the provision of services and the grocery chain benefits by offering a "special" service to its customers without the underlying, substantial, investment in hardware.

Increasingly, smaller organisations are providing connections between themselves at the local level. As an example two insurance companies might well do this to enable faster data exchange between themselves to facilitate claims enquiries and so on. This type of addition to the network structure is called a Commercial Internet Exchange (CIX) and these are likely to increase in number over the next few years. Figure A3 shows this, current, structure of the Internet.

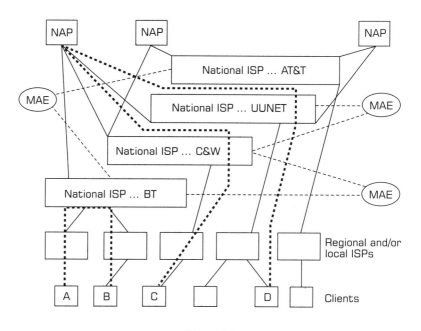

Figure A4

The final diagram (Figure A4) shows two alternatives in traffic flow. Clients A and B are two offices of the same company in two national locations. Imagine an office in London and one in Manchester. Their data would be routed through the network of their national carrier and would remain in this structure. This national carrier could easily offer them a very high-quality service since the majority of their data would be kept within the carrier's own network. Clients C and D represent an Internet user in one country and an associated supplier in another. Data flows from one machine into the corresponding carrier's system. From here it is routed through a NAP or MAE into the associated carrier, for the other side of the connection. After this the data travels to the recipient.

Clearly there could be more stages to this and in the first example a proportion of the total data traffic would remain in the "national loop" and some would travel across the "international loop".

The very flexibility of the current Internet structure will allow the production of a wide range of services offered by the major providers. Increased competition and demands from users for more and more bandwidth will mean a rapid evolution of this current physical structure with the production of more services and more varied physical connections into the Internet.

Some Useful URLs

It is impossible to give a definitive list of useful sources of information. The sites evolve and demands change. I have tried to give as wide-ranging a list as possible of sites that the relative novice to "The Web" might find useful. I have used many of these for some time and the fact that I continue to use them is sufficient evidence for their inclusion in this list. Some sites are included here because they represent the future of Internet shopping or Internet banking. This list is used as an illustration and is not meant to be exhaustive.

ISPs

Personally, I recommend BTConnect as an excellent home and small business ISP. They have a range of facilities set up for screening Internet access for homes and business. This means limiting the Web sites that a user can access –normally done to protect children from pornographic sites – but may also be employed to prevent a company's staff from unnecessary access to the Internet. In addition, they have the ability to register domain names and provide additional e-mail services.

```
www.btconnect.com
```

Search Engines

Make sure that you use more than one of them and get a feel for the type of searches that each one is best for.

```
www.netscape.com
www.yahoo.com
www.lycos.com
www.excite.com
www.altavista.com
```

Hardware Suppliers

There are many different hardware suppliers in the UK. Most offer good service and a good range of products. Here are two of my favourites:

```
www.scan.co.uk
www.insight.com/uk
```

Newspapers and Broadcasting Sites

```
www.telegraph.co.uk
www.thetimes.co.uk
www.bbc.co.uk
www.itv.co.uk
```

The BBC site is particularly good.

IT Updates, Software Downloads and IT Industry Information

www.cpmnet.com
www.zdnet.com
www.techweb.com
www.bhs.com (This is *not* the store!)

Internet Stores

www.amazon.co.uk
www.virgin.co.uk

www.tesco.co.uk
www.handbag.co.uk
www.harrods.co.uk
www.whsmith.co.uk

Banks and Building Societies

www.nationwide.co.uk
www.citibank.co.uk
www.halifax.co.uk
www.hsbc.co.uk

Glossary

Bandwidth A term used to describe how much data traffic (usually in bits per second – bps) can be carried down a wire in a network or the Internet. A bandwidth of 10 Mbps (megabits (million bits) per second) is faster than 56 Kbps (kilobits (thousand bits) per second).

Bridge A device which moves data depending on the MAC address of the data. Bridges are simple to setup but can produce inefficient networks.

Browser (1) A browser is a software program that allows a user to access a Web server

Browser (2) A browser (Microsoft's Windows network browser) which allows the user to see all computers on a network. It is called *Network Neighborhood*.

Client Usually a workstation computer that saves programs and/or files to a server.

Co-axial An older form of computer network cable which resembled aerial cable. An outer woven sheath covered a single data wire. The outer sheath provided considerable protection from electrical interference.

Cryptography The general process whereby data can be encrypted (hidden) so that non-authorised users have considerable difficulty in finding out what the contents contain. Cryptography refers to the principles and theory.

DHCP (Dynamic Host Configuration Protocol) A method of automatically setting up the TCP/IP configuration on a computer.

DNS (Domain Name Service) A method of resolving computer names to IP addresses.

Encryption The specific method whereby data can be encrypted (hidden) so that non-authorised users have considerable difficulty in finding out what the contents contain. Encryption is the "nuts and bolts" of the process.

Extranet   A network based on the TCP/IP protocols that allows selected outside users to connect into it by passing all traffic through a security mechanism (firewall) and refusing access to unwanted "visitors".

FTP (File Transfer Protocol)   This was one of the earliest protocols found on the Internet. It is used to move data and files around the Internet.

HTML (HyperText Markup Language)   This is a system of predefined tags or markers that are inserted into a document to change its appearance. HTML tags can affect the size of text, the appearance of text and the placement of graphics and links to other pages. It is extensively used in the World Wide Web.

Index Server   An index server provides a way of indexing all documents or files on a computer. It is intended to provide a corporate indexing capability across a wide range of computers. It works with the World Wide Web to provide searching and indexing capabilities for clients.

Internet   The Internet is a network of networks all of which use the TCP/IP protocols.

Intranet   An internal network (LAN) that uses the TCP/IP protocols.

IP (Internet Protocol)   One of the standard protocols (methods) by which computers can be addressed on a network. IP acts as the courier service in a TCP/IP-based data network.

ISP (Internet Service Provider)   This is a company or organisation that provides, for many people, an initial point of contact on the Internet.

POP (Post Office Protocol)   This provided local storage facilities for e-mail. The POP server would store the mail until the client contacted it and downloaded the e-mail onto their computer.

Proxy Server   A Proxy server allows a company to use their own (non-assigned) intranet and to connect to the Internet using this proxy server. The proxy translates the internal addresses into external (valid) addresses and in this way makes all communication with the outside world appear as if it is coming from the valid address.

Public Key   A form of encryption where two keys are needed to complete the encryption process. One key (the public one) is used to encrypt data. The other key (the private one) is used to decrypt the data.

Repeater   A device found on networks to clean and boost the electrical signal. A repeater carries out no processing.

Router   A device that moves data traffic from one subnet to another depending on the IP address of the data.

Search Engine   A program that searches for information on Web sites. This information is usually stored and maintained on a database. The search engine is run from your Web browser. Different search engines are good at finding different types of information.

SET (Secure Electronic Transaction)   SET is a very secure method of ordering and paying for goods over the Internet. It is cumbersome and unwieldy in use and many organisations have implemented a simpler and slightly less secure version. This simplified version still provides considerable security for most transactions.

Server   A general name referring to computers which offer "server services", usually they share files or printers on a network.

SMTP (Simple Mail Transfer Protocol) The standard method of moving mail from one computer to another.

SNMP (Simple Network Management Protocol)   A method of providing centralised control of computers using TCP/IP.

Switch   A device that functions like a fast bridge. It is used to build high-speed specialised networks.

TCP (Transmission Control Protocol)   TCP is responsible in a TCT/IP-based network for guaranteeing data delivery and data integrity on a network. TCP acts as the postal manager to IP's courier.

Twisted-pair   One of the commonest forms of wiring in computer networks. The system essentially uses high-grade telephone cables consisting of two wires wound together (twisted) so as to reduce interference.

URL (Uniform Resource Locator)   This is a reference in the form of

`http://www.ibm.com`

This is the way that Web servers are accessed and specific pages on a particular Web server can be reached.

WAP (Wireless Application Protocol) A range of methods whereby data and graphics can be delivered to the display of mobile phones.

Web Server   A Web server stores and makes available Web pages (HTML-based pages). A client connecting to a Web server will usually be offered the default page and from there will be allowed to navigate from one page to another by using the specialised links called *hyperlinks*.

WINS (Windows Internet Naming System)   This converts NetBIOS-based computer names into IP addresses.

World Wide Web   The Web refers to the way in which many servers are linked to each other through HTML hyperlinks. Nowadays "The Web" is synonymous with "The Internet".

147

Index